EVE'S GLUE
The Role Women Play
In Holding The Church Together

EVE'S GLUE
The Role Women Play In Holding The Church Together

Heather Wraight

First Published in 2001 by Paternoster Lifestyle
and Christian Research

07 06 05 04 03 02 01   7 6 5 4 3 2 1

Paternoster Lifestyle is an imprint of Paternoster Publishing,
P.O. Box 300, Carlisle, Cumbria, CA3 0QS, UK
and
P.O. Box 1047, Waynesboro, GA 30830-2047, USA
http://www.paternoster-publishing.com

Christian Research is the imprint of Christian Research,
Vision Building, 4 Footscray Road, Eltham,
London, SE9 2TZ, UK
http://www.christian-research.org.uk

British Library Cataloguing in Publication Data
A catalogue record for this book is available from the British
Library

ISBN 1-85078-418-3 (Paternoster Lifestyle)
1-85321-143-5 (Christian Research)

Cover Design by Campsie
Typeset by Westkey Ltd, Falmouth Cornwall
Printed in Great Britain by Cox and Wyman, Reading

To my mother, who taught me to love Christ, to enjoy writing and to have the courage of my convictions. Without any one of those this book would not have been written.

Contents

Foreword

I'll never forget my first experience of church. I was sixteen, on my way to a disco and dressed for the kill in a tiny glitzy number which barely covered my nether regions, panda eyes *à la* Dusty Springfield, and bright red PVC mac and hat which crinkled in the dirgical-liturgical silences. The hostile stares hardly made me feel at home and one swinging sixties teeny-bopper might never have gone back, never have become a Christian at all, had it not been for the post-service warmth of the welcome. It was unlike anything I knew I could expect from the cattle market of a disco.

Heather Wraight's experience made me reminisce. It's so easy to forget what it's like to walk in through those doors for the first time – the indecision, that clutch of fear in the pit of the stomach, the deep inhalation of breath, the strangeness of those unknown faces. And then, once we have become a part of the scenery, the frustration and bewilderment which months or even years later may make us walk out on our spiritual family.

The first church to which I ever really belonged told me, once I had married, that I now had one role in life – to bolster up my husband's ministry. Coming from a Jewish background I presumed that this must be the Christian way for women and tried to conform, until a combination of matriarchal genes, biblical study and reason prevailed. After several years of being defined in this role, I saw myself clearly one day as a rose in late autumn, limp, tired, with dying petals ready to fall to the ground. I knew then that if I was to survive emotionally and spiritually I had to get out. Fortunately we found another church, not nearly so lively, but much more accepting of a woman's gifts.

What attracts women to a particular church? Why do we feel comfortable in some, while others make us want to run? Why is attendance often sporadic, and what might make us leave altogether, despite the pain of cutting ourselves off from our community? These are hard, even threatening questions, but Christian men and women must face up to them if the church is to survive.

Heather Wraight will not let us shirk the issues, and she has all the power of statistical information behind her to hit us between the eyes when we're tempted to evade the truth. If prophecy is the calling of God's people to authenticity and integrity, then Christian Research, of which Heather is Deputy Director, has long been an important prophetic voice in our country, confronting us with the challenge of everyday reality.

Her fascinating stories, facts and insights, borne of years of careful research and listening to many women's experience of church, all demand that as a church we must think, grow and adapt. Women's re-lational gifts and love of community, our special ability to hold the disparate parts of the church together, have long been ignored and undervalued.

Eve ('Chava' in Hebrew) means 'life-force' or 'life-giver'. It has a verbal connotation. We were created to communicate life into our environment. In *Eve's Glue* Heather Wraight provides the evidence which proves the point, and invites us to acknowl-edge the unique resource women can be.

Michele Guinness

Introduction

'Women hold up half the sky' – Chinese proverb

Nearly half the people in the world are women. In Britain, they make up slightly more than half of the population. However, considerably more than half of those who attend church are women. Yet we do not know much about why they come to church, or why they sometimes leave. What is the most important aspect of their faith, and what do they enjoy most about church?

Soon after I joined Christian Research in 1994, a book called *Women in the Jewish Community* arrived in the office.[1] It had some fascinating material in it about Jewish women. I took it to our director, Dr Peter Brierley, and asked where there was similar material about women in the church. The answer, to my surprise, was brief – there was very little! Various research projects had looked at women in leadership, particularly with the long and vigorous debate in the Church of England about the ordination of women. Those with a feminist agenda had considered various aspects of church history and practice: 'As people have become more aware of the importance of the feminine in other aspects of society, they have also become aware of the lack of feminine input in major western religions.'[2] But of lay (non-ordained) women and the church? No, little was known. I was determined to find out!

A group of women interested in knowing more about women and the church was gathered together. Some of them were willing to form a steering committee under the chairmanship of Mrs Sarah Finch[3] while others became an advisory group. And so this research project was born.

The aims

The aims were clarified by the steering committee. We wanted to find out about the attitudes, needs and expectations of women in the church. In particular we believed it important to answer the questions posed at the beginning of this introduction.

We summed up our overall aim as _wanting to encourage women to play as active a part as possible in the life of their local church_. From the outset, we wanted to help lay women in the church rather than women ministers. We had planned a large, nationwide survey, but unfortunately we could not find enough funding to undertake this. However, the intention was always to publish the findings in a book, as well as to run some seminars based on the results.

This book

As I talked to people in focus groups and personal interviews, I asked them what sort of book they'd like. The response came down to 'something short, readable and not too expensive'. I'm not sure whether this book might be longer than what they had in mind, but I hope it will be readable enough to overcome that problem! To help illustrate the key points which came out of the research, and to earth the findings in the real world, I've created a fictional family. They are not meant to represent any specific people.

Books produced by Christian Research are often read by academics as well as ordinary churchgoers, so the kind of detail they want has been included, usually in the notes that conclude each chapter. Facts from other sources, which shed further light on the subject are added in shaded boxes. They are included for those who want more detail, but the book makes sense without them. At the end of the book there is detail of the methodology used, as well as a bibliography and a comprehensive index. Writing a book that is all things to all people is impossible, but I hope this comes close!

Heather Wraight

Notes

1   Schmool, Marlena and Miller, Stephen, *Women in the Jewish Community* (London: Women in the Community, 1994).

2 Puttrick, Elizabeth and Clark, Peter B. (eds.), *Studies in Women and Religion* Vol. 32, *Women as Teachers and Disciples in Traditional and New Religions* (New York and Lampeter: The Edwin Mellen Press, 1993).

3 A full list of steering committee members can be found on p. 200.

1

Why Bother?

Joanna and Stephen had moved house last week. It had been an exhausting affair, preceded by weeks of packing boxes, taking pictures off the wall and trying to decide where everything would go in their new home. Joanna sat in the middle of the muddle with a cup of coffee. She thought back over the last month and ruefully reflected that it had been all right for Stephen; he'd gone off to work in the morning and returned at night with a cheerful, 'Only six more days to go. How did you get on today?'

She'd been left with the kids and the mess. OK, the kids had gone to school, but not after bombarding her with questions.

'Will there be a Year 4 football team at my new school, Mum?', Andrew, a lively nine-year-old had asked – as if she would know!

'Can I really have a bedroom all to myself?' Louise, at seven, considered herself grown-up. 'And where will we go to walk Bessie?', she had asked, concerned for their elderly labrador dog.

Another of Andrew's worries had been, 'Will my new Sunday Club teacher be as nice as Ruth?'

This question prompted her soon-to-be-a-teen-ager, Matthew, to comment, 'If there isn't a decent youth group I shan't be going to church.'

Oh dear, why did it all have to be so complicated? It had seemed so obvious that if Stephen got the new job 50 miles away they'd have to move, if he was ever going to see anything of the children. The more they'd prayed about it, the more they were sure it was the right thing to do. The way they'd found the house and then sold their own at the last minute after the first sale had fallen through had all pointed to God's plan for them. Now they were here, and she didn't know what to do next.

Where was God in all the tiredness and hassle? She sat down with a cup of coffee and longed with all her heart for Nell to walk through the door. She really missed her friends, and she'd only been away from them since last Thursday. How would she ever find new friends like Nell, who always seemed to be there when she reached the end of her tether? Or Ruth, who was such a good Sunday School teacher that each of the children had come to a personal faith in Christ while they were in her class? What about Mary and Susan? They'd been a prayer triplet for about three years now and the friendship they'd developed in the process had been just as rewarding as the prayers they'd seen answered.

But it was no good sitting here moping. Last Sunday they hadn't gone to church; they were all too tired and grateful for the chance of an extra hour in bed. What about this Sunday? Come to that, what choice of churches was there in the town? She'd meant to ask their minister on the last Sunday, but somehow there had been too many people to say goodbye to. She had been so aware of what she was going to lose that future possibilities had been pushed out of her mind.

There must be several churches around here. They had to be in an Anglican parish; everyone in the country was, and in a town this size there would be other denominations as well. Steve had always been an Anglican, so naturally they'd gone to the parish church after they married. But she'd been to all sorts of churches, especially when she was away at college. She wouldn't mind being a Baptist or Methodist again. Andrew was very musical; perhaps he'd enjoy being in the Salvation Army's junior band. And at their last church some of the teenagers had gone off to join the large, enthusiastic youth group at the New Church which met in the local school – would that keep Matthew interested in church?

Bringing the children up in the Christian faith was not only something she wanted to do with all her heart; it was also a promise she and Steve had made when each baby was baptized. Finding a church where they could all be happy and grow spiritually was so important that she couldn't leave it to chance. She only had a week or two before she needed to start looking for a job. Church must get sorted out before then, if possible. Perhaps she'd better try to find out now what choices there were.

She dumped her empty coffee cup amongst the mess of unpacked boxes in the kitchen and called out, 'Come on Bessie, walkies. Let's go and find the library and see if they have a list of churches.'

* * * * *

FACT BOX

Moving home is one of the main reasons why people
change church. In 1992–3, 124,000 people transferred
from one church to another, the majority of them
because they moved house.[1]

Moving church

There are many reasons why people change church.
Moving house is one of the most easily understood
and accepted because it is seen as a positive reason.
In a later chapter we'll look at other reasons why
people leave. However, having left one church for
whatever reason, finding a new one is not an easy
matter. There are so many things to think about.
Here are some of the questions people wrestle with.

Does the new church have to be the same denomination?

The family's last church had been Anglican, but
Joanna in particular did not have a lifelong loyalty to
that denomination. Although she did not mind going
to another Anglican church, she was quite open to the
idea of trying another denomination, especially if its
local congregation offered what the family needed.
But for Joanna, that raised another question . . .

What does our family need from a new church?

Parents with children the age of Matthew, Andrew
and Louise are especially likely to consider whether

there is a Sunday School or youth group where the children will make friends. It is one thing for parents to want to continue to attend church, but they would really like their children to want to go with them. This is a strong consideration for Christian mothers, who often take the brunt of the unhappiness children may feel when they move home, lose their friends and have to cope with the strangeness of new surroundings.

Are there other people my age?

This is a question people of almost any age ask. When an elderly couple retire to a new area, they would obviously prefer if at least some of their new friendships were with other senior citizens – people with whom they can go out to coffee, or meet for other daytime activities. Parents want to make friends with people with similar interests and concerns, and for churchgoers one of the first places they look for those friendships is in church. It's important for children too – peer group acceptance is so vital in being able to grow up in your own crowd. For single people it is a key question, because making new friends who have common interests without someone 'matchmaking' can be quite a pressure.

The age of other members of the congregation also matters. Joanna thought back to the church she'd gone to briefly at college where the minister was getting on a bit and seemed as though he lived in another world. She pondered why she hadn't felt comfortable there, and wondered whether the age of the minister matters too.

FACT BOX

Ministers are more likely to attract people who are within 10 years of their own age.

What size of church do we want?

Some people feel at home in a large church, while others are wary of getting lost in the crowd. On the other hand, while it may be easier to get to know people in a small church, the warm welcome is often closely linked with delight at seeing another potential Sunday School teacher or new member of the choir. Joanna wanted to get involved in some role in the church, but she ruefully reflected that she didn't really want to find herself running the crèche from the second Sunday, as had happened at their last church!

FACT BOX

In 1998, 50% of the people who went to a Protestant church on an average Sunday in England went to only 15% of churches.[2] In other words, for half of English Protestant churchgoers their current experience of church is in a large congregation.

Do we want to worship within walking distance or are we prepared to travel?

This question arises particularly in a rural area. If the only church nearby is the local parish church, is it best to go and worship with local people, even if you're not an Anglican and feel uncomfortable with its style of worship? When I was a teenager, my parents chose to take my brother and me to a lively Baptist church seven miles away, because it had a thriving youth work and they wanted us to enjoy church. Once we had grown up my parents did attend the local church, and found themselves more easily understood and accepted as Christians by neighbours. For some people of course, travelling to church is not an option, perhaps because of poor health or lack of transport. Some women are more likely to have chosen to attend their church because it is close to where they live.[3] Perhaps some of them are among the many women who are 'church widows'– those who come to church alone or with their children and so they must go somewhere nearby so they can get home quickly afterwards.

What do *you* want from a church?

Have you moved house in the last few years? How easy was it for you to find and settle into a new church? What were the difficulties? Last time I moved I visited five or six churches over several weeks. I'd been very happy in my previous church, but recognized it was unrealistic to look for somewhere similar. There's a little saying, 'If you find the perfect church, don't join it because you'll spoil it!' It took me quite a while to work out what I really wanted from a church in this new area. As I tried out the local possibilities I realized that although good Bible teaching and a style of worship with which I could be comfortable were important to me, they weren't my top priorities. What I really wanted was somewhere where I could belong, make friends, and feel at home. I am not alone in coming to this conclusion, as I found when doing this research!

FACT BOX

Most women don't enjoy a new church until they feel they belong there (see chapter three).

If Joanna and Stephen and the children actually do make it to a church this Sunday, they will be consciously or subconsciously on the lookout for whether that church is likely to fit with their priorities. They are likely to ask questions such as:

- Is the worship a style we like, or at least a style we can be comfortable with?
- Was the sermon the kind we want?
- What sort of welcome did we get?
- Did the children like it?
- What activities beside Sunday services take place there?
- Did anyone notice we were there, and how did they react?

One woman told me about when she and her family moved to a new area. The church they started to attend had a lot going for it. But week by week the vicar shook hands at the door and said, 'Nice to see you. Thank you for coming. Please come again.' For six months they did 'come again', but he made no effort to get to know them, didn't ask their names or call round to see them. In fact, he didn't seem to realize that they had been before and eventually they stopped going. It would have been so easy for them to stop going to church altogether, but they believed that it was right to express their Christian faith by belonging to a local Christian family and to be part of the body of Christ in their area, so they looked for another church. Sadly they did not find one that welcomed them in that area, and at a spiritual level the family was greatly relieved when within a year they had to move again and could start church hunting in another town.

Why go to church?

This issue arises consciously or subconsciously throughout our spiritual lives, not only when we move. Even if you've been going to the same church for many years, why do you go there? When more than half the nation stays in bed on a Sunday morning, what makes you get up and go to church? The women I talked to listed the following reasons. Why don't you try putting them in priority order for yourself by numbering your most important reason as number one, the next as number two, and so on? Then ask other members of your family or your friends what order they would put them in. The list itself is deliberately in alphabetical order so it doesn't reflect the priorities of those who proposed the items!

Reasons why people might go to church

Reason	Priority			
	Mine	Other		
		1	2	3
The Bible tells us to	___	___	___	___
Commitment to a job there	___	___	___	___
Encouragement *from* others	___	___	___	___
Encouragement *to* others	___	___	___	___
Events and social activities	___	___	___	___
Example to children	___	___	___	___
Habit/convention	___	___	___	___
Meet friends	___	___	___	___
Meet with/closeness to God	___	___	___	___
'The only place I sing'	___	___	___	___
Sacraments, especially communion	___	___	___	___
See others grow spiritually	___	___	___	___
Space in a busy week	___	___	___	___
Teaching received	___	___	___	___
Time to pray	___	___	___	___
Use my gifts	___	___	___	___
Worship	___	___	___	___

Any other reasons?

_____   ___ ___ ___

_____   ___ ___ ___

_____   ___ ___ ___

Look at how you prioritized the list. How do you feel about it? Perhaps you struggled with whether you should put the more 'spiritual' items at the top of your list. If so, don't worry – that's how many churchgoing women feel! When they are being really honest, many of them admit they go to church primarily because of friendships and relationships. Their relationship with God is only one of the relationships they want to develop at church, although for the majority it is the most important. Friendships with and commitments to people they meet at church are also vital to most women.

Did you ask others about their priorities? If one of them was a man, was his order different in any way? Did he want to add other items to the list? Reviewing this list together with family or friends, or perhaps in a church home group, could make for an interesting discussion.

Relationships matter

This is one of the key findings of the research. Most of the women knew relationships were very important to them, but were surprised to realize just how crucial they are. One woman commented, 'I knew relationships at church are important for women, but I didn't realize just how important until I found myself thinking "relationship" as part of almost every answer I've given in the last hour and a half!' This is not saying that relationships are unimportant to men, but that they seem to give them a different priority.

How women build relationships is something we will look at in more depth in chapter three. But at this point it is important to examine what they want out of church, because a key factor in choosing a new church is assessing whether a particular congregation fits what we are looking for. We all know that no church is ideal, but secretly we would all rather like to find one which meets all our criteria!

Importance of a welcome

For women in particular one of the key issues is the welcome they receive, and whether the church is friendly. Why is this so important? According to Dr Deborah Tannen, most men are socially moulded to aim to be independent, to value individual achievement and to be competitive. In contrast, women often grow up being encouraged to connect with those around them, co-operating with them and emphasizing community.[4] Surely for Christians, church should be one of the places where those things can happen in a safe environment.

FACT BOX

A survey in Costa Rica in Central America looked at people who started going to a Protestant church and then left again within a few months or years. It found that while 10% of the population belonged to a Protestant church, 8.6% had previously belonged but had left.[5]

Unfortunately not everyone stays long enough to find out. We don't know the full nationwide picture for Britain, but we do for some countries.

If you are already settled in a church, what can you do to help newcomers feel welcome? One very simple thing is to speak to them! A colleague and I often work with a group of churches and try to visit each of them, unannounced, for a Sunday service. At one church the minister had told us he had a very friendly congregation but we happened to turn up when he was on holiday. He was horrified to be told later that as we went in we were given a hymn book and prayer book, but no one greeted us. It was an Anglican church, so we deliberately waited to see if anyone offered us the Peace – no one did. After the service we filed out without anyone speaking to us, handed back the books and left. Not one word had been said to us by anyone in the church. If we had been looking for a regular place of worship we almost certainly would have tried somewhere else the following week!

Some people are excellent at spotting visitors. A friendly word of welcome, an explanation of where the loos are and what's available for their children if they've come too can make all the difference to whether those visitors come back again. It may even change their whole life, as Michele Guinness related in the Foreword. In one large church we surveyed, 38% of the women said that they had chosen that particular church because it had a caring congregation, compared with only 22% of the men.

Meeting needs

The main reason for attending church for all of us,
young and old, men and women alike, probably
ought always to be because worshipping with others
is part of what it means to be a Christian – the writer
to the Hebrews encouraged Christians not to 'give
up meeting together' (Heb. 10:25). However, our society is much more individualistic than it used to be
and it's no longer acceptable to go to church simply
because we ought to, or out of duty. There must be a
desire to want to attend, and for many people that includes having their personal needs met.

The Southwell Diocesan Social Responsibility
Group carried out some research in 1992 among
twenty women who had left the church, as part of the
diocesan response to the World Council of
Churches' Ecumenical Decade of Churches in Soli-
darity with Women. The book is a compilation of
quotes from the women, and many of the comments
they made would be echoed by women still in the
church, for example:

'If you're going to go to church on a regular basis,
it's got to be one that suits your needs and meets
your needs,' and,

'If we are going to have a church and it's going to
be effective, it's got to meet people at their point of
need.'[6]

Look again at the list of priorities we considered.
How does that translate into needs? Here are some
suggestions:

Priority	Need
The Bible tells us to	Desire to obey God
Commitment to a job	To take an active part in the church
Encouragement from others	Affirmation and support to keep going
Encouragement to others	Help others to keep going also
Events and social activities	Belong to a community
Example to children	A desire for them to share my faith
'I feel wrong if I don't'	Habits of a lifetime give shape to life
Meet friends	Relationships
Meet with/closeness to God	Without this I might as well join a club
'The only place I sing'	Some things are more enjoyable in company!
Sacraments, especially communion	Nourishment to keep faith alive
See others grow spiritually	Makes witness or service feel worthwhile
Space in a busy week	Moments of 'oasis' are precious
Teaching received	Learning should lead to spiritual growth
Time to pray	Praying with others is helpful
Use my gifts	Play my part in church
Worship	To enjoy God and his presence

You may want to word some of these 'needs' differently, but it is quite clear that at church we are looking for a mixture of the spiritual and the practical. This links in with the old discussion of whether you can be a Christian without attending church. Many people, of course, think you can. But they are missing out on so much; not only the receiving of teaching and spiritual nourishment, but also on being able to use their gifts 'so that the body of Christ may be built up' (Eph. 4:12). Without being able to give and receive encouragement and participate in corporate prayer and worship our spiritual life is poorer, and maybe not fully Christian.

'Fellowship' has humorously been described as 'fellows (men and women!) in the same ship' – we are all in the same boat. If we don't attend church, we're going it alone spiritually. So why go to church? Because it enriches our lives enormously, not only spiritually but also at many other levels. This is especially true for women, because it is here that we make the friendships that nurture and sustain our Christian faith.

FOR FURTHER THOUGHT

1 What Joanna missed most from her previous church were the friendships, while Andrew missed his Sunday Club teacher. What would you (and your family if you have one) miss most if you were to move away from your present church?

2 Look again at 'Reasons why people might go to church' on page 10. If you want to discuss this

list with other people but haven't yet done so,
write down here who you will talk to and when:

Who _____ When _____

Who _____ When _____

Who _____ When _____

Who _____ When_____

3 Try to describe the sort of church where you
think Joanna and her family would be happy.
How would it be different for you, and why?

Notes

1 Brierley, Peter and Wraight, Heather (eds.), 'Introduction', *UK Christian Handbook 1996/1997* (London:
Christian Research, 1995), pp. 26–7.
2 Brierley, Peter, *The Tide is Running Out* (London:
Christian Research, 2000), p. 49.
3 Christian Research, *Congregational Attitudes and Beliefs
Survey* pilot study, 1998, p. 14.
4 Tannen, Deborah, *You Just Don't Understand: Women
and Men in Conversation* (London: Virago, 1992).
5 Gómez, Jorge, 'Protestants in Costa Rica', *They Call
Themselves Christian* (London: Christian Research,
1999).
6 Miles, Rosie, *Not in Our Name: Voices of Women who
have left the Church* (Nottingham: Southwell Diocesan
Social Responsibility Group, 1994), p. 38.

2

Who Are The Women?

Joanna sat gazing out of the window, thinking hard about what they should do about church. They'd tried several now, and the family just didn't fit in. She remembered that disastrous first attempt. They'd been very tired after the move, and so had decided to go to the little chapel around the corner. She'd known the minute they walked in that it was the wrong place for them, but you couldn't very well turn round and walk out again, could you! Matthew had looked at her with a mixture of disgust and horror as an elderly woman attempted to welcome him with, 'Hello, son! It's lovely to see you. We haven't had any children here for a long time.' They'd endured the service, and made polite noises about 'wanting to find the right church' as they escaped as quickly as possible afterwards.

The next Sunday they'd tried a church she'd discovered in her walks with Bessie. It had looked reasonable from the outside, even though the notice-board was a bit tatty. But it did say that there was a Sunday School, so they'd gone along with high hopes. The Sunday School had turned out to be little more than a way of keeping the children occupied during the adult service. Afterwards, she discovered that Matthew had taken himself off to the local park to play football and hadn't been to the Sunday School at all. Andrew had stayed put, but he'd pleaded not to go there again because there was only one other boy among the eight or ten youngsters.

Joanna was beginning to realize that choosing a new church was nothing like as easy as she'd expected. Their last church had been fairly full on a Sunday, with a couple of hundred people of all ages. She'd assumed that most churches were like that, but certainly not the ones they'd been to so far. She didn't want to go somewhere with a congregation of mostly elderly ladies – nothing against them; she was sure the church was a great comfort for them, almost like a family. But she wanted to be able to make friends her own age. She also knew that a church like that would mean Stephen would either finish up doing far too much at church, or not coming at all. And above all she wanted to find somewhere where the children could make friends and find encouragement and help in their Christian faith.

* * * * *

FACT BOX

Churchgoers are older than the general population. Their average age is 43 years compared with 38 years for the general population.[1]

Most of us know intuitively that women are different from men. The popularity of books like *Men are from Mars, Women are from Venus*[2] shows how eager people are to understand those differences. This book highlights the ways in which we behave, but there are other, more measurable differences, both in society at large and in the church. Being aware of some of them helps in understanding the issues women in our churches are wrestling with.

The numbers

It may surprise you to know that among younger people (under 45 years of age, which is middle age as defined by the statistics people) there are more men than women in Britain! Here's how it works out.

Table 1: *UK population in thousands, 2001*[3]

Age	Number	% Female
Under 15	11,288	48.5
15–19	3,727	48.6
20–29	7,469	48.9
30–44	13,747	49.6
45–64	14,086	50.5
65 or over	9,301	59.5
Total	59,618	50.8

These statistics reflect the sad situation that men die younger than women; 500 women are widowed every day in the UK.[4] In 1993, three quarters of a million women in the UK were aged 85 or over, and a girl born in that year could expect to live to be 79.[5] Looking around practically any church congregation on a Sunday confirms that there are more older women than older men, but not that there are more younger men than women! The overall age and gender pattern in churches is somewhat different from society in general, as this table shows.

Table 2: *Age and gender profile of churchgoers in England, 1998*

Age	Population			Churchgoers		
	Men %	Women %	Total %	Men %	Women %	Total %
Under 15	10	9	19	9	10	19
15–19	3	3	6	2	4	6
20–29	7	6	13	3	6	9
30–44	11	12	23	6	11	17
45–64	11	12	23	9	15	24
65 or over	7	9	16	10	15	25
Total	49	51	100	39	61	100

You don't have to be good with numbers to see immediately that there are more women in church than men in every age group. However, if you look at the middle column on each side – the percentage of women in the population and in church – you can see several factors:

- There were more girls than boys in church in England in 1998, but in the population there were more boys than girls.
- Only in the 30–44 age group was there a lower proportion of women in church than in the population.

- From age 45 onwards there was a much higher proportion of women in church than in the population.
- The proportion of men in church aged 20–44 was significantly less than in the population and still somewhat less in the 45–64 age group.
- The proportion of men in church was only higher than the population once they reached 65 or over.

In other words, older people and women are over-represented among churchgoers, compared with the general population. This isn't only because women live longer! Some might say that the higher number of women in church is due to women being somehow more 'spiritual', or perhaps more intuitive than men – there are a number of arguments both for and against this, which we'll consider in chapter eight.

So what do all these numbers mean? In sheer numbers, women are the backbone of the church. In the Muslim religion, only the men go to prayers at the mosque. Just imagine how empty many churches would be if only the men attended!

Births, deaths and marriages

Births

Children are brought into the world by women, and even in the era of 'new man' are mostly brought up by them as well. There was a mini baby boom in the

UK in the late 1980s, as those who were born in the big baby boom of the 1960s started to have their own children.

Table 3: *Births, 1970–96*[6]

Year	Number of births	Births per 1,000 population	% Births outside marriage
1970	903,900	16.2	8
1975	603,400	10.7	9
1980	753,700	13.4	12
1985	750,900	13.2	19
1990	798,600	13.9	28
1995	732,000	12.5	34

In theory, the increase in births in the late 1980s ought to mean there are more children in church in their pre and early teen years. In fact there are in the church I currently attend. What about yours? What implications does this mini baby boom have for activities such as Sunday School and church youth work? Large numbers of teenagers left church in the 1980s, and there was such concern about it that several Christian organizations working among young people did a major research project[7] and then put in place strategies to try and retain young people. They've had a measure of success, in that the drop-out rate was much less in the 1990s. However, much more worrying is the huge number of younger children we've lost in recent years.

The other factor in table three is the massive increase in the number of babies born to unmarried mothers, who may be single or cohabiting. In 1993,

25% of divorced women and 23% of single women were cohabiting,[8] and the percentage has grown since then.

Table 4: *Percentage of churchgoers in each age group, 1979–98*[9]

| | Population | | | Churchgoers | | |
| | 1979 | 1989 | 1998 | 1979 | 1989 | 1998 |
	%	%	%	%	%	%
Under 15	21	19	19	26	25	19
15–19	8	8	6	9	7	6
20–29	14	16	13	11	10	9
30–44	19	20	23	16	17	17
45–64	23	22	23	20	22	24
65 or over	15	15	16	18	19	25

Unfortunately, many children decide they've had enough of church around the time they move to secondary school, or during their early teenage years. As the larger numbers who were born in the late 1980s reach that decision point, can we take action that will keep more of them in church? Many Christian mothers with children like Matthew would dearly love to be able to. Various Christian organizations working amongst children and young people are also working hard at this.

Changing patterns of family life

There are now 1.9 million households made up of cohabiting couples in the UK.[10] 25% of all non-married people aged 15 to 59 and 39% of those aged 25 to 29 are currently cohabiting, which is a factor many churches are having to face up to. Such people often feel uncomfortable in church.

When a Christian family breaks up, anecdotal evidence suggests that some family members will stop attending church. The growing number of children who are living with only one of their parents, usually their mother, is almost certainly another factor behind the drop in church attendance by children. If they come to church at all it is more likely to be with their mother, or even their grandparents. However, if Sunday is 'daddy's day', church is unlikely to feature in the programme.

These changing patterns have theological implications. For example, the traditional Christian theological position is that any sexual relationship outside marriage is wrong. The arguments for and against that position, on biblical, social and compassionate grounds continue to be debated furiously in religious, academic and political circles. However, in day-to-day practice the question is not initially whether or not these people are 'living in sin', to use the old-fashioned phrase, but whether we are able to welcome cohabitees if they come to church and, if so, can we help them feel they belong? What extra support and encouragement can the church offer single mothers? And how can parents help their own children make wise choices about such ethical dilemmas? This isn't the place to try to answer such questions, but we certainly have to be aware of the issues and think through our responses to them.

Yet another reason for the decline in church attendance among children is the decrease in the frequency of attendance. Now, only about half of all

churchgoers are in church on any one Sunday, and if
Mum and Dad take the day off to visit Granny, go to
the seaside, or do the shopping, the children are ex-
tremely unlikely to come to church on their own.

> **FACT BOX**
>
> 7.5% of the population are in church on any one
> Sunday, but this is not the same 7.5% as will be there the
> next Sunday. 10.2% of the population attend church on
> Sunday at least once a month.[11]

This changing pattern of attendance also has practical implications. For ministers it has all sorts of re-
percussions:

- If someone only comes to church once a month,
  how do you spot if they aren't there because
  they're ill?
- What do you do about a series of sermons if
  some of the congregation only hears one in four
  of them?
- How do you help people to feel they belong if
  they aren't there very often?
- Are there ways of keeping less regular attenders in touch? e.g. Mrs Smith may have died and
  the funeral taken place since they last came to
  church.

It also has implications for members of the congregation:

- A Sunday School teacher may have two in the
  class one Sunday and nine the next, so how
  much material does he or she prepare?

- Children may find they hardly ever meet certain other children in their group, because they are rarely there on the same Sunday.
- It can be easy to slip into the habit of not going to church every Sunday, and so for attendance to gradually become less and less often without realizing it.
- If an adult does not attend regularly they are much less likely to want to take on a regular job, whether that is serving coffee, teaching Sunday School or welcoming people as they arrive.

However, although only about 7.5% of the population of England can be found in church on any one Sunday, that doesn't mean the church has no place in people's lives. Nearly half of all babies are still baptized in church during their first year of life. The reasons for this are very varied, and include:

- Everyone in the family has been baptized,
- If anything should happen to the baby, he or she will have been baptized,
- So that the baby may belong to the church,
- To give the baby a name in a proper ceremony,
- Because one or both parents were born a Catholic.[12]

Marriage

Almost every girl dreams about getting married. In my childhood, the dream that I enacted with young friends as we raided the dressing-up box was always a white wedding in a beautiful church. One of the benefits of the parish system in the Church of England is that so many people who normally have no contact with the church nevertheless opt for a church wedding.

Weddings are one way of establishing contact with people who do not regularly attend church. Many ministers and vicars take the opportunity to talk to those who request a marriage service, not only about the commitment they are taking on, but also about the significance of making vows before God. People under 30 getting married for the first time are still more likely to choose to marry in a church rather than anywhere else. Not all denominations permit divorcees to marry in church, and this reduces the number of church weddings of older people. The number has also decreased since it became possible to get married in a wide variety of locations, provided the venue has been registered. In 1994 there were 297,000 marriages in the UK, but only 113,000 of them were 'religious' marriages (i.e. in a church or another place of religious worship).[13]

A couple I knew had a life-changing experience as they took their vows, each of them suddenly realizing that they were making promises to a God they did not know. They agreed that one of their first priorities in their marriage was to find out about him. That might not have happened if their wedding had not taken place in church.

Old age

As the population figures in table one showed, men are more likely to die before women. There are many more widows that widowers in this country – nearly two thirds of women aged 75 or over are widowed.[14] This has many implications for a woman. She is much more likely to be living on her own in old age than a man is, whether or not she has been married. The traditional 'women's meeting', many of which are often attended by women who do not attend church on Sunday, seems to be dying out. But the number of older women in the population and in church suggests there is still a place for such gatherings. They offer older women the opportunity to meet and talk to others with common interests, as well as to receive spiritual help and encouragement.

An older woman is also more likely to have to cope with the death of a spouse. Even in this age of low church attendance the vast majority of people still opt for a funeral with a religious dimension, either in a church or a crematorium chapel. This may bring people back into touch with church after a gap of many years. Research among older people found that bereavement is a key reason why older people start coming to church, although for others it causes them to leave, perhaps because attending alone a place they have gone to as a couple for many years is too painful.[15] The high number of widows in church inevitably has pastoral implications for churches, as they seek to support and help those of their number who have lost their partner of many years.

These 'occasional offices', as the church calls baptisms, marriages and funerals, are very much family occasions. They also bring many people, who may have little other contact, into the orbits of the Church of England and Roman Catholic Church especially.

They therefore present excellent opportunities for building on the tenuous links which keep people coming back for such events. 63% of the people of Britain would call themselves Christian. When they come to your church for a baptism, wedding or funeral, what impression do they receive?

Such events are usually big family occasions. How can we who are inside the church rather more often encourage the people who come to these events to visit the church at other times and not only at a major point in their lives? Some churches run follow-up programmes, visiting the homes of babies who have been baptized, offering bereavement counselling, or inviting relatives of those who have died to attend an annual service to mark the anniversary. It often seems to be women who get involved in such ministry. For some it is not only because they care, but also because they have more time available. However, that too has changed in recent years.

Women and work

The number of women who go out to work increased enormously in the twentieth century. In 1994, half of all adult women in the UK were employed either full-time or part-time, and by 1997, 71% of women of working age were in employment.[16]

The number of women who are 'economically active', that is in paid employment or registered unemployed, has changed in the past 30 years. Fewer 16–19-year-old women are in this category now (65%

Table 5: *Economic activity by age, 1994*[17]

	Working full-time %	Working part-time %	Unem-ployed %	Econo-mically inactive %	All women (100%)
16–19	17	26	9	48	1,300
20–24	49	13	8	30	2,000
25–34	41	24	6	29	4,600
35–44	36	35	5	24	3,900
45–54	37	34	4	25	3,600
55–69	23	29	4	44	1,500
60–64	7	18	1	74	1,500
Total[a]	27	22	4	47	23,300

[a]Includes those aged 65 and over

in 1971, 58% in 1996), almost certainly reflecting the increased numbers staying on at school or going to college. The drop among the 60–64-year-olds probably shows more women retiring on time or early, rather than continuing to work after retirement age. However, in all the other age groups the percentage has increased, especially for those between 25 and 44, the age of most mothers of young children.[18]

What does this mean for church life? Simply that fewer women are around during the day. Organizations that seek specifically to evangelize women have found that their pattern of events has had to take account of this. Coffee mornings and luncheons,

Table 6: *Changes in women's economic activity by age,
          1971–96*[19]

	16–19 %	20–24 %	25–34 %	35–44 %	45–54 %	55–69 %	60–64 %	Total[1] %
1971	65	60	46	60	62	51	29	44
1996	58	69	73	78	77	56	27	54

[1] Includes those aged 65 and over

all the rage 20 years ago, now attract fewer women of
working age in most places. This isn't necessarily
because of lack of interest, but because the women
who might have been willing to come can't – they're
at work. And when they come home they cannot easily drop everything to go out to a church meeting, as
many of them are still carrying the bulk of responsibility for running the home.

I must admit to finding some things in the above
table quite amusing, such as women eating their
meals eleven minutes quicker than men – do we all
leap up to get on with the washing-up while the men
are finishing their final cup of tea?! But where is the
time for church activities, especially for those who
are working? It becomes an even bigger question
when you look at the fine details.

FACT BOX

British women work harder for less money, have more
children, head more one-parent families and die sooner
than any of their counterparts in Western Europe.[20]

Table 7: *Time usage for adults in Great Britain, 1995*[21]

	Minutes per day		
	All	Male	Female
Paid work			
Paid work	168	212	127
Labour services			
Travel	46	50	43
Unpaid work			
Food preparation	49	28	68
Care of family/household	71	55	86
Clothing care	14	3	25
Shopping etc.	36	26	46
Care of home	56	43	70
Total domestic current	**226**	**155**	**295**
Self-improvement	27	33	21
Home improvement	14	22	6
Total domestic capital	**41**	**55**	**27**
Work for others unpaid			
Voluntary work outside the household	13	11	15
Consumption/leisure			
Sleep and rest	536	533	539
Leisure	226	226	226
Eating	141	146	135
Exercise and sport	229	38	20
Total leisure/eating	**396**	**410**	**381**
Total consumption/leisure	**932**	**943**	**920**
Other			
Other	7	7	6
Missing	7	7	7
All activities	**1,440**	**1,440**	**1,440**

Table 8: *Division of household tasks by couples*[22]

	Always woman %	Usually woman %	Usually man %	Always man %	Together %
Washing and ironing	48	32	1	1	18
Deciding what to eat	28	33	1	1	37
Looking after sick in family	24	28	0	0	48
Shopping for groceries	20	21	4	1	54
Small repairs	2	3	51	26	18

What kind of jobs do women in Britain do? In 1987, 1% of those working were in agriculture, 18% in industry and 81% in services.[23] A slightly different way to look at it is by what proportion of people working in each job category are women.

This shows that many women who work have responsible positions as teachers, in the health service, or other similarly demanding jobs. This can create two opposite reactions when it comes to taking on responsibilities at church: either 'I've got enough to do already, thank you very much,' or 'Why can't I do more than make the tea?' We'll look at such issues in chapters five and seven.

Table 9: *Percentage of each job category held by women, 1986*[24]

	%
Professional and related occupations in science, engineering, technology	9
Professional and related occupations in education, welfare and health	69
General management	11
Clerical and related occupations	74
Catering, cleaning, hairdressing and other personal services	76

Behaviour of women churchgoers

Several other research projects by Christian Research in recent years revealed interesting information about women churchgoers. Many of the following facts come from a survey of nearly 2,500 people in 1995,[25] the majority of whom were churchgoers. As you would expect, many of the findings only underlined things that we already knew, either from the media or by personal observation, for example:

- Women were more likely to be employed part-time than men.
- Men were twice as likely as women to be involved with sport as a leisure activity (31% men, 15% women).
- The percentages were almost exactly the opposite for going shopping as a leisure activity (30% women, 17% men).

- Women were more likely to be involved in church activities (72% women, 62% men).
- Men and women liked watching different things on television. Men watched more news than women (87% to 69%) and also watched more sport than women (44% to 17%), while women watched more soaps (43% to 18%), drama (63% to 46%), documentaries (55% to 49%) and game shows (17% to 10%) than men.
- A few more men listened to BBC radio than women (67% men, 63% women), while independent local radio attracted more women than men (21% men, 14% men).

What was surprising was that so many questions about behaviour were *not* answered differently by men and women! So, for example, there was no difference between how honest men and women were, what kind of sexual lifestyles they found acceptable, or how much confidence they had in various social institutions. There were much bigger differences reflected by age or social class than by gender.

This was also true of most questions in a survey of social concerns for churchgoers of one denomination.[26] However, there were some interesting variations by gender in this research, for example:

- It was more important for women that they should have pleasant workmates (29% of women, 14% men).
- Women were less keen than men that newspaper editors should report scandals involving publics figures (32% men, 19% women).

Such figures tend to underline the common belief that women are more 'people-related' than men.

There is little to do with gender to be gleaned from these surveys, and perhaps that in itself is interesting! We might think that men and women churchgoers have very different attitudes about society in some areas, but when those attitudes are actually tested they prove remarkably similar. What practical implications does this have in church life? Well, it means that looking at social issues perhaps in a home group or a midweek meeting is just as likely to be of interest to women as to men.

There are also hints here of other factors. Women get their information from slightly different sources from men, which may mean a different perspective on the same piece of news. And we really do like different leisure activities! So laying on separate activities for men and women, at least from time to time, may not be sexist but rather catering to our varied needs and interests.

What women believe

An important survey of the attitudes and beliefs of churchgoers has so far only been done as a pilot survey in a small number of churches – 20 churches attended by 3,000 people – so it is not possible to generalize. Therefore as you read this section you may well think, 'I'm not like that,' or 'It's not like that in my church.' It will be fascinating to see if the patterns this pilot survey reveals are true across the country.

So what did it show about women in those few churches?

- When asked how they had come to faith, whether by a gradual process or a definite moment of commitment, men were more likely to have had a specific time of commitment (66% men, 54% women).
- Women were much more likely to sense the closeness of God in worship. Nearly two thirds of the women questioned said that they always or mostly sensed God's closeness in worship, compared with only half of the men, and more of the women said they always felt that way (16% women, 11% men).
- Nearly half (45%) of the women said their faith had grown much during the previous year (compared to 31% of men).
- Women were more likely to have a private devotional time most days (70% women, 54% men). The average man in this survey had a private devotional time on 211 days a year, while the women averaged 246 days – nearly a month's difference!
- Women supported children's charities far more than men (52% women, 40% men), while the same proportion of men (52%) gave to evangelism (against only 36% of women).

So what does this survey tell us? Do women experience faith in the same way as men? Not necessarily. However, they certainly experience church differently, which is the subject of the next chapter.

FOR FURTHER THOUGHT

1 Does your church follow the pattern that Stephen and Joanna found of having many more older that younger attenders? If so, do you know whether anyone is thinking about the implications? If not, who or what has made the difference?

2 How welcoming is your church for people like single mothers, divorcees or cohabiting couples? Are you satisfied with your answer? If not, could you do anything about it?

3 Does your church do anything to keep in touch with people who get married there, or who come for the baptism or funeral of a family member? Could you be involved in this in some way?

4 You are probably aware of the differences in lifestyle between your generation and your mother's generation. If your own mother is a churchgoer, have you ever talked to her about how the differences have affected your involvement in church?

Notes

1 Brierley, Peter, *The Tide is Running Out* (London: Christian Research, 2000), p. 94.

2 Gray, John, *Men are from Mars, Women are from Venus* (London and New York: HarperCollins: 1993).

3 Brierley, Peter, *Religious Trends 2000/2001* (London: Christian Research and HarperCollins*Religious*, 1999), table 4.3.

4 Ibid. table 4.8.1.

5   Whitmarsh, Alyson, *Social Focus on Women* (London: HMSO Central Statistical Office, 1995), table 3.28, p. 48.

6   Brierley, Peter, *Religious Trends 1998/1999* (London: Christian Research and Carlisle: Paternoster, 1997), table 4.7.

7   Brierley, Peter, *Reaching and Keeping Teenagers* (London: MARC Europe, 1992).

8   Whitmarsh, *Social Focus on Women*, p. 13.

9   Brierley, *Religious Trends 2000/2001*, table 12.3.5.

10 Christian Research, 'Trends in Cohabitation', *Quadrant*, July 2000, p. 3.

11 Brierley, *The Tide is Running Out*, p. 77.

12 Christian Research, private research for the Church of Scotland, 1998.

13 Brierley, *Religious Trends 2000/2001*, tables 4.7.1 and 4.7.3.

14 Whitmarsh, *Social Focus on Women*, p. 10.

15 Christian Research, *Older People and the Church*, private research for the Sir Halley Stewart Age Awareness Project, 1999.

16 Department for Education and Employment leaflet, *Equal Opportunities – Women*, 1998.

17 Whitmarsh, *Social Focus on Women*, p. 21.

18 These figures are equivalent to the total of the first three lines of table 5, although they are for different years.

19 Whitmarsh, *Social Focus on Women*, p. 21.

20 'European Lifestyles', quoted in *The Times*, 25 June 1996.

21 *Radical Statistics* 74, Summer 2000, table 1, p. 20.

22 Johnston, Philip, 'Society shows its more feminine side', *Daily Telegraph*, 22 October 1998.

23 Eurostat, *Women in the European Community* (Brussels: Eurostat, 1992), p. 82.

24 New Earnings Survey 1987, quoted in 'Women at Work', *Sociology Update* (London: DfEE, 1989).

25 Christian Research, *Ansvar Survey of English Social Behaviour*, 1995.
26 Christian Research, *Church and Society*, private survey for the United Reformed Church, 1996.

3

Count Me In!

They'd been here for six months now, Joanna reflected as she sat in the home group bible study. What had they achieved? Well, the house was pretty much sorted out – there were hardly any boxes left in the garage now, and she suspected the few remaining ones would probably still be there next time they moved!

The children all seemed fairly happy at school. Matthew had found it difficult to join Year 8 in the middle of a term, but he was now involved in several of the after-school activities and was trying for the under-14s cricket team. He didn't tell her much, but he talked to Stephen when they went fishing together. To her great relief, he had decided 'for the time being' to come to church with them, and one of the lads from his Sunday morning bible study group was in the same year at school.

Andrew and Louise were easier to please, and, after an initial couple of incidents of name-calling, they'd found some friends and settled into the routine of life at junior school. She and Stephen would soon have to think about a secondary school for Andrew, hopefully somewhere with a good music department.

Moving hadn't made much difference to Stephen, who still went off to work as usual, and he'd never had many friends outside work. There was a computer group at church and he'd been along to that a couple of times. He must be fairly happy because last week he'd suggested they start giving regularly to the church by standing order. He wouldn't want to give like that if he wasn't expecting to stay there for a while.

But what about her? Here she was sitting in this group of people whose names she knew, but how much more did she know about them – or them about her for that matter? She looked around at them, and suddenly realized that they were nearly all married. There was Joyce, whose husband had died recently, and Clive, a mildly eccentric middle-aged bachelor whom everyone humoured. Joanna thought about her new work colleagues – half of them seemed to be separated or divorced, and often living with a new partner. But there were no such people in this group, and she realized that people with those kind of lifestyles probably felt less than welcome in most churches.

She'd tried hard to stop comparing the folk in their new church with her old friends like Nell, Susan and Mary, but there was still a massive gap in her life. After trying a couple of churches which didn't feel right for them, the family had been warmly welcomed from the first Sunday at this church. That had been very significant in their decision to settle there and she had almost immediately felt she could find a spiritual home among these people. But how did you get beyond that?

It wasn't helped by the fact that she'd been able to get a job fairly easily and was working as a receptionist-cum-personal assistant at a small engineering company just off the high street. It was OK as jobs go, and brought in the money they needed to help with the mortgage. The difficulty was that she was so much more tired now she was working full-time than in her old part-time job. She hadn't the energy left to have people round to dinner, and she was at work when the church badminton club met.

She looked around the room at the dozen or so men and women in the home group. They were nice enough people, but would she ever feel she belonged here? How did that happen anyway? What was it that turned an acquaintance into a friend? She thought about her next door neighbour, Christine. They'd got on well right from the start, and had been able to talk openly about their Christian faith from the first time Chris had invited her in for coffee. It had come as quite a surprise when Chris admitted she hadn't been to church for two or three years, except for the school carol services and a friend's wedding. One day she'd have to ask Chris why she'd stopped going, although right at this moment she thought she could probably understand.

Joanna suddenly realized that the prayer time had finished and someone was talking to her.

'We're having a barbecue on Saturday, would you and the family like to come?'

'Yes, that would be lovely, thank you. Do you want me to bring anything? I presume it's OK for the children to come as well?'

'Of course the children can come, and it would be great if you could bring a salad. Do you know where we live?'

Perhaps this would be the way she could start really getting to know some people. All the others seemed so at home with one another, and it suddenly occurred to her that they'd probably be surprised if she told them how out of it she felt. She decided she really did want to make the effort to get to know these people better.

* * * * *

> **FACT BOX**
>
> An important part of belonging in a church is to have friends there.

What does belonging mean?

One of the questions researched was, 'What does it mean to say you "belong" in your church?' Although the women came from very different kinds of churches – various denominations, large and small, rural and urban – the answers were remarkably similar. They were much more to do with relationships and acceptance than with spiritual reasons.

Being known

For many women it is important that people know them by name – to be Joanna, not just Stephen's wife or Matthew's mother, or even 'that new woman'! It helps with a sense of identity, which psychologists tell us is often weak in women. It gives a warm feeling to walk into church after the hassle of getting the children ready in time and the dinner in the oven, and to be greeted personally. For someone living alone, Sunday morning may be the first time they've spoken to anyone since coming home from work on Friday evening, and for widowed or divorced people conversations at church may be the only meaningful ones they have face to face all week.

Not all of us are good with names, of course, but at least we can admit that! It is much nicer to be welcomed with a relevant comment or question – 'So glad to get to know you a bit at the barbecue last night' – than to be ignored because of embarrassment about a forgotten name.

Being valued

However, being known goes deeper. It is about being valued as a person, not just a 'bum on a pew'. It is being welcomed for whoever I am, and without reservation. I live in Eltham, just a mile or so from where Stephen Lawrence was murdered. Although that happened before I moved here, the inquiry had a personal relevance because the crime occurred locally. One of the main findings was 'institutional racism' in the Metropolitan Police, and immediately there were questions in the Christian press about whether the church was racist.[1] Those who came to Britain from the West Indies in the 1950s and 60s, as Stephen's parents did, would undoubtedly answer that it was then. Many of them found no welcome in the predominantly white churches where they hoped to find a spiritual home in a Christian country that was their new physical home. The result is that in our inner cities, especially London, some of the most vibrant and fastest growing churches are black majority churches. Indeed, in inner London, just over half the churchgoers are non-white – they are mostly black Africans and Caribbeans but with a good mixture from South Asia as well.[2] What might it have meant for church life in Britain if those immigrants had been welcomed and made to feel they belonged?

These days, there are still many in society who often feel less than welcome in church: single parents, divorced people, cohabitees, homosexuals, the unemployed, the less well educated, those who have difficulty reading, the mentally handicapped, and others who unfortunately feel marginalized by the church as well as by society. In fact, just the sort of people whom Jesus Christ went out of his way to meet, such as the woman at the well (Jn. 4:1-26). Coming to church for the first time, or the first time for a long time, is a daunting experience. Anyone who makes the effort to cross the threshold surely should receive a warm welcome – and go on receiving it – even if there are aspects of their lifestyle or experience which we personally find hard to accept.

FACT BOX

In Australia, the national census asks a question about church affiliation, so they have a better idea than we do in Britain about who does and doesn't go to church. Almost every group is under-represented in comparison with their proportions in society – young people, single people, married people, the less well educated and second generation immigrants.[3]

Feeling accepted

This is a very important part of what goes on to make
that feeling of belonging. It is quite hard to describe,
but women use phrases like 'I feel part of the family,'
'I feel at home,' and 'I can be myself without being
frowned at.'

Penny Jamieson, the Bishop of Dunedin in New
Zealand, was the first English woman to be appointed an Anglican bishop anywhere in the world.
Even in that senior position, acceptance and belonging were key issues for her: 'It is a question of how
we claim belonging, of whether or not we can assert a
position of validity on the inside . . .'[4] Her book, *Living at the Edge*, is primarily about the leadership role
of being a bishop, its demands on her and the lessons
she has learned which she uses to help other ordained women. In this context she writes:

> It is not uncommon for women, as they present them-
> selves as candidates for ordination, to stress how well
> they have been 'accepted' by people who have begun to
> see the signs of vocation in their lives. This is associated
> with the *general tendency that women have to emphasise the
> relationships they have with others, the support they have re-
> ceived from other people and the regard in which they are
> held*. (Italics mine.)[5]

Being accepted goes much deeper than being welcomed and for some people is a more significant factor in feeling they belong. Think back to Joanna's
reflections. At one level she felt she now belonged to
that church – she and her family would probably

happily say to neighbours or friends that they now belong there. They attended regularly, had become involved in activities and were talking about giving to the church. But she did not feel really accepted yet; she wasn't 'on the inside'.

There are four questions that people ask, often subconsciously, when they first join any new group and these seem particularly relevant to a woman's need to belong to a church.

- *'Who am I?'* Joanna might ask herself whether she was the newcomer, the fat or thin one, or the only one with or without a bible at the group that night. She might also question whether she had a right to be there; perhaps it seemed from the conversation as though nearly everyone in the group went through the same Alpha course a couple of years ago, or were all at school together.

  'Who am I?' also involves asking, 'Who do I have to be to become accepted here?' Does Joanna share all she knows from her years of being a Christian, and so be seen as an 'expert' who might be useful to the group, or does she keep quiet so people have to draw her out? If the 'Who am I?' question is not answered, Joanna will remain hesitant, fearful of committing herself, and find it difficult to trust herself to the others.

- *'Who are you?'* Not only what are your names, though that is a good start, but where have you come from? What is your personal story? Where are you on the journey of faith? Are you all people who have been Anglicans all your lives, like Stephen, or are some of you secret rebels, wanting to try a different denomination or style of worship but not quite knowing whether you should? Perhaps some of you are secretly considering dropping out of church and the demands that faith makes. Does anyone here long to change their job? Or does anyone carry enormous responsibilities, like caring for elderly relatives?

What does Joanna need to know about the others in order to trust them, to begin to open up to them and join in the group fully? And what do they need to know about her? How will that knowledge be shared – in a formal question and answer session, or during conversation at the barbecue, or picked up in bits and pieces from what people say or the kinds of things they pray about? If 'Who are you?' remains unanswered, it will be hard for Joanna to make decisions about her place in the group, or to join in wholeheartedly when they are considering action.

- *'What are we here for?'* This question might be very specific to a particular meeting, but it also needs a wider answer. Home groups meet for different purposes in different churches, so if Joanna thinks she's come for bible study, while everyone else is there to work towards evangelizing their street, there will be a mismatch of expectations. When she realizes her misunderstanding, it may come as a relief or a shock, and could lead either to her abandoning the group because she doesn't identify with its aims, or subconsciously fighting to try and turn those aims into something closer to her own. If a group is not in agreement about what they are there for, it can either become very competitive, with everyone battling to get their own ideas listened to, or apathetic as people opt out.

Different churches also have different cultures and very varied atmospheres and expectations. For some churches the priority is worship, while for others it is evangelism. In some, the atmosphere is contemplative and reflective and worshippers are expected to participate quietly in whatever way they wish. In others there is a sense of excitement, and participation in some obvious and perhaps vocal way is expected. Taking a noisy toddler to a meditative style of service can be asking for trouble, with the family anticipating being able to worship together, while others present want to be able quietly and reverently to come into the presence of God!

- *'How are we going to do it?'* What are the rules round here? Should I take a Bible? Will I be acceptable in my work clothes or should I change? Have I sat in the seat that Mrs Jones considers her own? Learning the ways of doing things is easier if someone explains them. Perhaps people take it in turns to bring cake to have with coffee – being told that will make it much easier for Joanna to feel free to offer to bring one next time.

New people in a group wonder who really is the leader – is it the person who introduced

themselves as the leader, or is it someone else
who usually gets their suggestions accepted?
The ground rules may be decided by an individual, the group, or on a wider basis. So if it's
the vicar who decides what the church's home
groups will study there isn't much point in
complaining to the person leading that evening. However, if there are no ground rules, a
'free-for-all' can lead to power struggles as
those with clear ideas try to get their own way.

Ask yourself these questions in relation to a group
you belong to, whether it's an official one such as a
church home group, or an unofficial one such as a
bunch of friends. The answers you give will probably reveal a lot about how well you feel you belong in
that group.

Being involved

Women want to be involved, not just spectators at
church. Whether they make coffee, teach Sunday
School or become minutes secretary to the PCC (Pa-
rochial Church Council, the local governing committee of an Anglican church) is in one sense irrelevant.
A job in the church, whatever it is, gives a sense of
identity. This is two-way, because very often taking
on a specific job or role in the church brings someone
more closely into contact with a few people whom
they can then quickly get to know much better. For
most of the women involved in the research, this desire to be involved was strong, even if their lives
were already very busy. Those who were not

involved in some way, however small, felt themselves on the outside, looking in on all that happens but not really a part of it.

In some parts of Africa there are multitudes of small, indigenous churches. New ones are constantly being formed, and part of the reason is that everyone wants to be involved and thus have their own identity. So one person is the prayer co-ordinator, while her sister is the assistant prayer co-ordinator, the prayer co-ordinator's husband may be the stewardship secretary, her sister's husband the treasurer, and so on. Once the church grows too big for everyone to have a role, it is highly likely that some of them will leave and form a new church.[6] This is perhaps taking involvement to an extreme, but most of us are much more comfortable when we have a specific role. This level of involvement also gives everyone a sense of security, responsibility and status, which are attributes many churchgoers would probably welcome more in their church. It may also be a factor in why there are so many black churchgoers in Britain, especially in London.[7]

God has called you there

For some people there is a very strong spiritual sense that a particular church is the right place to be. Not everyone would want to use the word 'called', a term that is perhaps more frequently used among evangelicals. However, the same conviction about the rightness of worshipping in a particular church is experienced by people from many church traditions.

This aspect of belonging may be linked, for some people, to feeling a strong sense of God's presence in a particular church, but more of that later.

FACT BOX

In one survey, a sense of belonging in church was strong only for those who attended at least once a month. Those who went less often than they used to reported that their sense of belonging was weaker than it used to be.[8]

Joanna and Stephen knew that it was right to move, although they did not have the same deep, inner conviction about which church to attend. One woman I talked to took temporary accommodation when she moved to a new area until she found which church she wanted to join. Only then did she look for somewhere permanent to live, near the church. This inner conviction is very important for some people, and if it is missing they may feel uneasy.

One danger highlighted by the research is that we may judge whether people really belong by our own criteria. So if, for example, I have a strong sense of conviction that this is the church where God wants me to belong, I may feel that someone who doesn't have that conviction is not fully committed. One of the enormous strengths of the church is that in theory (or theology!) at least, its doors are open to everyone. But in practice that's unfortunately not always true.

How quickly does belonging happen?

There are clearly two levels of belonging for women. The first usually happens quite quickly. It is a sense of feeling comfortable, of knowing that this church is one where I could throw in my lot. It is the right place to be, and offers the potential of what I am looking for in a church. It may give a warm welcome, or provide opportunities for Christian service, practise the kind of worship I want, or be the nearest congregation of the denomination to which I belong. For whatever reason, something 'clicks' and it feels OK to explore further.

For most women that happens fairly quickly, sometimes on the very first visit. For some people that is enough, but others are looking for something deeper; a sense of being part of a community, of being really locked in to a network of friends and activities. When I first moved to Eltham I did not want to rush into choosing a new church. Working for a Christian organization which serves church leaders of many denominations, I thought it would be helpful to visit most of the churches in the area to experience worship and patterns of Sunday services with which I was not very familiar. However, after three months or so I wanted to settle down somewhere. I wanted to walk into a church on Sunday morning and not be a visitor. This first level of belonging is when that sense of being a visitor has passed, and a conscious or unconscious decision has been made to come back here regularly.

The second level of belonging is the one Joanna was still struggling with after six months. It is the deeper sense of feeling really at home, and it commonly seems to take up to a year or even longer. For some people, particularly if they are wary of committing themselves for any reason, this aspect of belonging may take much longer or may never happen at all. It can be particularly difficult for a vicar's wife – one commented:

> People in a church want a relationship with the vicar's wife, not with you as a person. That means it takes much longer for you to feel you belong than it does for your husband, and he may not understand that at all.

Who needs to belong?

For most women the desire to belong is a motivating factor for throwing in their lot with a local congregation. For some in particular, belonging is a strong need.

The newly widowed

We saw in chapter two that the church has many widows among its worshippers, as well as some widowers. As one senior citizen widow put it,

> The church is a place where widows are honoured and dignified in a way that is rare in society.' Grief is a painful and lonely process, but having supportive friends around is one of the most helpful ways of

moving through the anger, guilt or other aspects of bereavement. To become whole again after the loss of a loved one, perhaps after many years of marriage, is a difficult task. For a bereaved person it is important to have a safe place where they can learn to be a single again; somewhere where they are accepted and appreciated for who they are and not only for what they were.

The single

This group may never have married, or be widowed people who have come to terms with bereavement. The issues they face and the support they might welcome from church will vary. For example, the biblical standard and long-term teaching of the church is that sexual relations should only take place within marriage. For younger single people trying to live by that standard in a world where many around them choose not to be celibate, it's enormously supportive to belong somewhere where that stand is affirmed and understood.

Older single people living alone who do not go out to work may have little meaningful contact with other people. An elderly neighbour of mine goes shopping at least once and sometimes twice a day, partly because it gives her something to do, and partly because at the shops she is among people. She doesn't go to church, but another bereaved neighbour who does finds some longed-for companionship there. For single people who are in employment, the conversations and contacts at work may be superficial, only related to the job, or even quite stressful. Church can be a good place to drop the role required at work, leave behind the pressures, and relax.

FACT BOX

In 1992, 35% of all adults attending church were single.[9]

Unfortunately, some churches give single people the impression that they are not whole people if they haven't got 'another half', and singles have not always had as much understanding and support from fellow Christians as they deserve.[10] It can be harder for a single person to fit into a new community when they move, particularly if they work long hours and perhaps also commute to work. Some people make new friends at the local sports club or pub, while others also want to do so in the local church!

Young mothers

Members of this group may well feel the need to belong, especially if their own mother lives a long way away. Many adults in our mobile society live miles away from their own parents. If Joanna and Stephen ever did live near either of their parents, they certainly no longer do so now they've moved to a town 50 miles from where they last lived. Distance stretches and changes the sense of belonging to a family, and church can become a substitute, with all the pluses and minuses of any family! This is particularly valuable for mothers, for whom life can feel very restricted if they are at home with young children. Parent and toddler groups or home groups are run in many churches during the day, and are a great way for mums (and some dads!) to get out and make new friends.

In Britain an increasing number of mothers return to work within a few months of their baby being born, and these mothers face different pressures. Understanding friends can be a help at such times, and church may be where they meet those friends regularly.

> **FACT BOX**
>
> In 1997, 71% of women of working age (16-59) were economically active – in other words, in paid work of some sort.[11]

The 'downside' of belonging

Although there was almost unanimous agreement among the women in the research about their desire to belong, there were some negative answers to the question 'What does it mean to you *as a woman* to say you belong?' The difficulties revolved around other people's – mostly men's! – expectations of what role they would be comfortable in. Joanna hoped she would not be expected to run the crèche from her second Sunday in the church, and that kind of expectation is not uncommon. In some churches, especially small ones which are desperate for help, you can hardly walk through the door before you are pounced on. Someone is sure to see you as the answer to their need for another Sunday School teacher, a new person for the tea-making rota, the alto that they are missing in the choir or worship band, or suitable for any one of the dozens of practical jobs which need to be done in a church!

Other women find almost the opposite. They decide on a new church, and feel full of enthusiasm about using their gifts to serve God in that context. And then they run up against people in the church, possibly the leaders (although not necessarily), who are uneasy about women taking on certain roles. We'll look at some of these issues later, but a woman who encounters such attitudes can find it much harder to settle down and feel she really belongs.

Relationships of whatever kind always bring problems as well as joys: 'When we examine relationships between people, we discover the difficulties and pains that tempt one to flee into the desert, as well as the value of these relationships.'[12]

Helping others to belong

Belonging seems to be one of the key factors in how much women commit themselves wholeheartedly to the life of a church, and therefore to service for God within it. Because it is important for women to feel they belong, they are often more than willing to encourage others to belong also. This may be by means of evangelism – drawing others into the church and to a personal faith in Christ. In one study, women were more likely than men to come to an Alpha course because they were invited to attend by a friend or relative.[13] Women may be more comfortable building friendships *within* the church. It seems that it's very often the women who do the running in relationships within the church, and it's in this sense that they are the glue which holds the church together.

*   *   *   *   *   *

. . . But count me out!

Chris settled down with the mug of coffee that Joanna had just given her. They'd chatted to each other on several occasions in the months since they'd been neighbours. But finding time for a long talk had been more difficult. Two or three times a year Stephen took Matthew out fishing, and today Andrew had gone with them for the first time. Louise had been invited to join a school friend on a birthday outing to Alton Towers, and to Joanna's delight had been eager to go. She was glad to see her youngest child growing more confident after the unsettling time when they first moved and, having met the child's mother and assured herself that the day was properly planned, she'd been very happy about the invitation.

As soon as Joanna realized that she had a whole Saturday to herself, she'd phoned Chris to invite her round, and had been thrilled when Chris immediately accepted. They talked about all sorts of things for quite a while – their jobs, the weather, the forthcoming local election – and then Chris casually asked if the family were happy at church.

Joanna was immediately struck by the way Chris phrased the question. Ever since she'd discovered

that her neighbour had a strong Christian faith, but
hadn't been to church for two or three years, she'd
wondered why. So that was it – she hadn't felt happy
at church.

Gradually the story came out. It was a combination of various issues. Chris had been attending the
same church since she was a teenager, and over the
course of time it had changed in lots of little ways.
Each individual change hadn't mattered that much,
but one Sunday as she had walked in Chris felt as
though she was a stranger. She had realized that very
few of the friends she'd grown up with in the church
were still there. Nearly all of them had married, and
relationships had subtly changed, especially when
children came along. Some had drifted away from
church and she had lost contact with them. One or
two had gone to university and hadn't come back afterwards, while others had got jobs in other parts of
the country. When they did occasionally come back
to visit their families they greeted Chris warmly, but
they hadn't time to come and spend an evening with
her in the house she'd so happily bought for herself.

Her job was much more demanding now too, and
sometimes she had to be away on business. It irked
her when people asked if she'd had a nice holiday
when all she'd seen was the inside of a conference
centre. She didn't have quite the same energy at 45
that she'd had at 25, and it was really rather nice to be
able to stay in bed on a Sunday morning rather than
rush out to get to church in time to set up for Sunday
School. Because 'good old Chris' was always willing
to take on jobs, she'd realized that fateful Sunday
that she no longer went to church to worship God,

but only because of what she was expected to do. The next Sunday she'd found someone else to take her Sunday School group and gone for a picnic in the country. She had sensed God's presence there in a way she hadn't felt at church in a very long while. She hadn't meant to drop out of church, but she'd just never gone back, and it hurt that no one seemed to care that she had stopped going – she didn't even get a phone call asking if she wasn't there because she was ill. What made it worse was that she didn't really miss church, and as she looked back on her years of faithful attendance she realized that for several years she'd gone out of a sense of duty and habit, and to be honest had often found it boring and irrelevant.

Joanna sat there thoughtfully, wondering if anyone had really listened to Chris's story before and simultaneously asking herself how many more people like Chris there were.

* * * * *

FACT BOX

For every person in church on an average Sunday there are four who used to come regularly and no longer do so.[14]

Leaving church

People leave their church for a range of reasons, most of them, unfortunately, ones that show the church up in a bad light. Surprisingly few stop going because they have lost their faith.[15] One of the most common reasons is that church is irrelevant, and closely linked is finding it boring. Some drop out when they move and either do not make the effort, or are unable to find a church to join in their new area.

If you've been a member of a church for any length of time, you can almost certainly think of people who used to be very committed, but who no longer come. Research among those who attended ecumenical Lent groups in 1994 and were attending church at that time found that up to half of them had dropped out of church for at least a year at some time in their adult lives.[16] Among the groups of women who gathered to discuss *Women and the Church*, nearly half had had at least a year out, for a variety of reasons:

- Pre-school children made church such a hassle one woman didn't go back until her children were at school.
- Another became bored with the style of worship, left intending to find somewhere else but didn't do anything about it for a while.
- Frustration at not being able to use her gifts in a church which didn't believe women should take on leadership roles led another woman to leave.
- Some went to university and, having been to church with their parents all their lives, made their 'own choice' and didn't go for several years.
- Another's husband didn't want her to go.

- One family moved home and couldn't find a church they liked.

Obviously, many of those who leave are women, though we do not know exactly what proportion. However, there have been at least two research projects, one in Australia and one in the UK, which have looked specifically at why some women leave church.[17] They came to startlingly similar conclusions. One point in common was that few women had been able to talk about their experience to anyone in the church, especially not to their minister or vicar.

In Australia, nearly all the women interviewed had been deeply involved in church life. In a group who were all aged between 33 and 43, the average length of time they'd been attending church was 20 years, so they'd been going for much of their lives. They had previously seen their church involvement and Christian faith as vital and central to their lives. They had all been dedicated leaders or members of bible study groups, some had held responsible administrative positions in their churches and in Christian organizations and four had studied theology.

The UK study didn't go into quite the same detail about the church involvement of those who had now left, and those interviewed were from a wider age range. Nevertheless, each came to similar conclusions. As the foreword to the UK study puts it: 'Women leave the Church, not because it expects of us more than we can give, but because it does not expect enough.'[18] In both groups, women felt that they constantly had to fight against the inferiority which the church institution imposed upon them.

Many of these women were highly intelligent, with responsible jobs. The contrast between work or academic study and church became impossible. The women in these studies didn't leave because they'd given up on their Christian faith, but because they felt stifled by the institutions. They were no longer comfortable trying to live within what they saw as constraints placed on them by the church:

> Each woman had spent many years faithfully believing, or trying to believe, that she should relate to God in particular ways prescribed by church leaders, and by the doctrinal and theological statements of the church. But each, in her own particular circumstances, began to find that difficult.[19]

No longer belonging

In other words, they no longer felt they belonged as they once had. As one of the Australian women put it, 'Movement out of the church meant great freedom, a release from pressure and conformity.' They described their difficulties as being 'disillusioned', or 'not being allowed to be human.' One woman commented, 'I would have hoped that the Church was a safe place to be oneself, but I actually don't find that it is. It's a place of great condemnation.'[20]

One of the greatest dangers of the sense of belonging is an expectation that everyone should conform. When the criteria for belonging to their church seemed to exclude the possibility of 'being human', these women eventually rebelled. Most of them did not lose their faith, and some remained friends with people who still attended their previous church. But they stopped attending.

In the *Women and the Church* research I didn't set out to find out why women leave. But I came across three who fitted the pattern of these two studies. They had each been deeply involved – one had been the wife of an Anglican vicar, another a deacon in a Baptist church, and the third helped to lead a Christian organization. These are women the church cannot afford to lose, and yet it has – at least for the time being. Are you in danger of becoming one of them? One woman wrote this poem:

> *Ma Raison D'être*[21]
> _____
>
> *– to think the unthinkable,*
> *– to dream the impossible,*
> *– to perceive the potential,*
> *– to risk the unknown.*
>
> *– to unlearn the learned,*
> *– to learn the unlearnt,*
> *– to disarm the abled,*
> *– to enable the disabled,*
> *– to venture . . . beyond,*
> *– to create something – beautiful,*
> *– nay, . . . – useful,*
> *– nay, . . . – fruitful,*
>   *for . . . God?*

Coming back

The women in our study who had left church for at least a year all returned. What had brought them back? For some of them it was what is sometimes called a 'crisis of faith'. They met with God afresh, through many and varied circumstances, and that new or renewed relationship with God drew them back to wanting to worship him with others.

For most, however, the main reason was a human relationship of some kind. One came back because her mother encouraged her to do so. Another was deeply touched by the care and help she received from people in her previous church when her marriage broke up. One returned because her vicar phoned her up and persuaded her she was just the person to do a particular job! Others discovered that the freedom they thought they had found did not turn out to be as rewarding as they had hoped. The reason most often given was that a woman missed her friends at church, the fellowship and the sense of belonging.

Is there someone you ought to phone right now? Someone who used to come to your church, but who no longer does? Perhaps she needs to hear that you haven't forgotten about her! You never know, she might be missing that sense of belonging – to God as well as to a church.

FOR FURTHER THOUGHT

1 By now Joanna felt accepted in their new church, but not yet that she really belonged. Do you have a sense of belonging in your church? Is it

stronger or weaker than a year ago? What do
you think are the reasons for your answer?

2 For Joanna, starting to feel she belonged began
when the family were invited to a barbecue.
Could you organize an event for your church (or
group within it) that would help people feel they
belong more?

3 Joanna was concerned about the expectations a
new church might put on her. Do you have similar concerns? Have you ever talked about them
to anybody?

4 Have you ever felt like Chris? Or do you know
somebody in her situation? Who is offering you
or them the sort of support Joanna gave to Chris?

Notes

1 e.g. *Baptist Times*, 4 March 1999, p. 3 and *The Church of
England Newspaper*, 5 March 1999, p. 5.
2 Brierley, Peter, *The Tide is Running Out*, (London:
Christian Research, 2000), p. 139.
3 Hughes, Philip, 'Nominalism in Australia', in *They
Call Themselves Christian* (London: Christian Research
and Lausanne Committee for World Evangelization,
1999), p. 33.
4 Jamieson, Penny, *Living at the Edge*, (London: Mowbray, 1997), p. 30.
5 Ibid. p. 34.
6 Brierley, Peter, *Future Church* (London: Christian Research, 2000), p. 133.
7 Brierley, *The Tide is Running Out*, p. 138.
8 Christian Research, *Older People and the Church*, private research for the Sir Halley Stewart Age Awareness Project, 1999.

9   Evangelical Alliance, *Singularly Significant* survey, 1992.

10   These issues are explored extensively in my book *Single, the Jesus Model* (Nottingham: Crossway, 1995).

11   Department for Education and Employment leaflet, *Equal Opportunities – Women*, 1998.

12   Ocho, Carol, *Women and Spirituality* (New Jersey: Rowman & Allanheld, 1983), p. 114.

13   Simmonds, David, *Training for Change in the Church* (unpublished MA dissertation), 1998.

14   Richter, Philip, and Francis, Leslie J., *Gone but not Forgotten* (London: Darton, Longman & Todd, 1998), back cover.

15   Fanstone, Michael, *The Sheep that Got Away*, (Eastbourne: Monarch, 1993).

16   Brierley, Peter, *Finding Faith in 1994* (London: Christian Research, 1994), study for Churches Together in England.

17   Diesdendorf, Eileen, 'Why Some Bright Women Quit the Church', *Zadok Perspectives* No.21, 3/88 and Miles, Rosie, *Not in Our Name: Voices of Women who have left the Church* (Nottingham: Southwell Diocesan Social Responsibility Group, 1994).

18   Miles, *Not in Our Name*, p. v.

19   Diesdendorf, 'Why Some Bright Women Quit the Church', p. 2.

20   Ibid.

21   Reproduced with kind permission.

4

His-Story, Her-Story[1]

Joanna snuggled down into bed and opened up the book she'd been given for her birthday. It had a section on women in church history, and last night she'd decided she'd make a start on it today. She'd succumbed to the very heavy cold that had been going around at work. They'd told her to go home yesterday, 'and stay there until you've stopped spreading all those bugs around!' She was usually disgustingly healthy, so the chance to have a day off work – even with a very good reason – was not to be sniffed at. Or rather, as she was still sniffing appallingly, she'd make the most of the day off! She hadn't slept very well because her cold meant she couldn't breathe easily. As she lay awake, trying not to cough so she wouldn't wake Stephen, she'd tried to think which women she'd heard about from church history.

In recent months her experiences of church had made her think about issues she hadn't considered much before. She found she was feeling increasingly strongly about the role of women in the church. She'd realized that the comparative freedom she'd enjoyed in the churches she'd attended was not shared by all churchgoing women, whether in other churches, different parts of the world or at other times in history.

The Bible wasn't too difficult. Even in the Old Testament there were women such as Miriam (Ex. 2:4, 15:20,21, Num. 26:59), Moses' sister, who'd fascinated her when she took the children to see the film *The Prince of Egypt*. She'd remembered mothers like Rebekah (Gen. 24; 27:1–17), who'd helped her favourite son Jacob to cheat her older son out of his birthright, or Sarah (Gen. 18:1–15), who'd famously laughed (Gen. 18:12) when she heard visitors from God telling her husband Abraham that she'd have a son 'this time next year' (Gen. 18:10).

The New Testament was easier. There was Mary of course, with her key role as the mother of Jesus (Mt. 1:18–25, Lk. 1:26–56; 2:1–40). When Mary and Joseph had taken their baby to the temple to be circumcised they'd met the elderly Anna (Lk. 2:36–38). When you'd been going to church for several years, as she had, you'd certainly heard one or more sermons on Martha and Mary (Lk. 10:38–42). Funny how when a male vicar looked at that story he usually had so little sympathy with Martha – how would he feel if thirteen hungry men turned up on his doorstep and he had to cook for them?! There were the nameless women, like the Samaritan at the well (Jn. 4:1–42), or the woman caught in the act of adultery (Jn. 8:1–11) – how had the man escaped being brought to justice if they had been actually caught at it? There was the other Mary, Mary Magdalene – after all she'd lived through, what an incredible privilege to be the first to see the risen Jesus in the Garden of Gethsemane (Jn. 20:1–18). At that point she must have dropped off to sleep, and her dreams mixed up Gethsemane and Mary with her own garden and Stephen's despair at the state of the grass after only one summer of Matthew and Andrew's football.

Joanna rarely had peace and quiet to read – three children, a husband and an elderly dog made sure of that. That morning she'd coughed and spluttered her way through the morning chores: packed lunches for three, walked Bessie, made sure there was something in the house for dinner tonight and superficially tidied up once the children had left for school.

She flicked through the pages as she sipped a lemon and honey drink. How come she'd never heard of most of these people? She read avidly. Here was Perpetua, a 22–year-old from Carthage in North Africa. She'd refused to renounce her Christian faith even for the sake of her baby son, and was martyred in AD 205. The fact that she wrote her own story until being condemned to death shows she must have been an educated woman, and therefore probably from a wealthy family. Joanna thought back to when Matthew was a baby. She'd still been in her twenties, and she would have done almost anything for him. The thought of this young woman's death, leaving her baby motherless, nearly moved her to tears.

Marcella was the next woman to catch her attention. She was a wealthy Roman woman who, when she became a Christian in the fourth century, turned her palatial home into a Christian retreat house. In

AD 382 she invited Jerome – ah!, she'd heard of him – to teach in her home while he was in Rome working on the Latin translation of the Scriptures. Jerome recognized Marcella's grasp of Scripture, and was amazed that things he had learned through long study and meditation she had learned without anyone to teach her. He was so confident of her understanding that he once asked her to settle a dispute between bishops and presbyters in Rome about the meaning of a certain passage of Scripture. Marcella had apparently become the leader of a large circle of influential women who wanted to follow Christ and be obedient to him amidst the high society of Rome. Joanna wished she could have been at the bible studies in Marcella's house, and pondered that the basic problems couldn't have been so very different for those women than they were for her – how to maintain Christian standards and values in a Godless society.

She read on. Another gifted woman of the same era was Paula, a young friend of Marcella. She was from an aristocratic family who owned the city of Necropolis. But her wealth hadn't saved her from heartache – her husband had died young, leaving her with five young children. Joanna reflected on what it would have meant to bring them up alone, and what she might have done in similar circumstances. This wealthy young widow became a Christian at Marcella's Bible studies, where she also met Jerome. Eventually she went with Jerome to the Holy Land, where she helped in his translation work by paying his expenses, including buying ancient books and rare manuscripts for him. She studied Hebrew and learned to speak it fluently, and went on to found four religious houses, three for women, and a hospice where she and her sisters cared for the pilgrims, the sick and the needy. How had she found time to do all that as well as bringing up five children? Having money no doubt helped; she would have had plenty of slaves to help her. But no, the book told her that Paula had lived simply and given away her possessions to help the poor and needy. She must have had endless energy as well as a deep commitment to serving God!

So there were women's religious orders as early as the fourth century – that surprised Joanna. She knew vaguely about convents in the Middle Ages, and last year they'd visited Whitby in North Yorkshire while they were on holiday. Hilda had been the abbess there, and a pretty amazing woman she must have been![2] Apparently bishops, kings and princes all used to seek her advice, and yet ordinary people were still welcome to come to her. It was in her abbey that the Synod of Whitby had taken place in AD 663 and 664.[3] This Synod had brought together representatives from two opposing parties from the early days of Christianity in England: bishops appointed by Rome, whose spokesman was Wilfrid, and Celtic bishops, who by then had taken up residence on Lindisfarne (or Holy Island) as well as Iona, and whose case was put forward by Bishops Colman and Chad. They'd had to decide whether English Christianity would follow Celtic teachings, or accept the Roman teachings and papal rule which were fairly universal across Europe. The particular matter which precipitated it all was how the date for celebrating Easter should be calculated. To Hilda's great disappointment, they'd decided on the Roman method, and Joanna wondered what might have happened to the church in Britain if they'd chosen to keep the Celtic traditions.

Another woman from the same period in British history, Ethelberga, came to her mind. When Augustine arrived in Kent in AD 597, one of his early converts was Ethelbert, the King of Kent. Ethelberga was one of his daughters. Around AD 625 King Edwin of Northumbria sought an alliance with Ethelbert, and asked for Ethelberga in marriage to seal the agreement. This was turned down because he was not a Christian. He replied that Ethelberga would have complete freedom to practise her Christian faith, and so the marriage was agreed. Ethelberga wanted to take Paulinus, her own chaplain, with her on her journey north, and before they left he was consecrated the first bishop of York. Paulinus' desire was not only to help Ethelberga remain faithful to Christ, but also to see the Northumbrian people become Christians. Pope Boniface was very interested in this missionary enterprise, and wrote long letters both to Paulinus and Ethelberga. On Easter Day AD 627 King Edwin was baptized, along with many of his fellow Northumbrians.

Joanna discovered that Ethelberga had been one of several queens who had played an important role in the early expansion of Christianity. Catherine of Alexandria, Queen of Egypt, had been in the process of bringing Christianity to her country when Emperor Maximinius invaded. When Catherine's ability to defend her faith resulted in some of his own leading scholars converting to Christianity, he wiped out all the Christians. Another influential royal was Princess Olga, who had ruled the Kiev region of Russia in the middle of the tenth century. She was given the credit for making the first steps towards establishing the Christian church in Russia.

Hildegard of Bingen, from the twelfth century, was another revelation to Joanna. Well educated, she knew the Scriptures, could speak and read Latin and had been taught natural science and philosophy. She obviously was not a meek and mild personality who willingly submitted to men in authority. If she saw something she believed to be wrong, she did her utmost to put it right, including writing indignant letters to church leaders, despairing over the corruption of clergy. She made her views very clear, often with such positive results that she was regarded as a prophet 'by everyone from Bernard of Clairvaux and the Pope, down to the humblest labourers'.[4] But she also had a sensitive side, and wrote at least 77 liturgical songs as well as producing a treatise which was in effect a theology of music.

Now here was someone else Joanna had vaguely heard of, Julian of Norwich. She remembered as a teenager when she went on a sailing holiday on the Norfolk Broads that they'd visited Norwich. The small room where Julian had lived her life of solitary silence and prayer had seemed rather weird to Joanna then. As a teenager she couldn't imagine anyone wanting to shut themselves up on their own for most of their life. But now as she read about Julian's writings and the close relationship with God from which they stemmed, she realized that this must have been a woman with a very special faith. In the fourteenth century she had expressed that faith in a way that showed her depth of commitment. What would be the equivalent today?

There was a bark from downstairs, and Joanna was jolted back to the present day. She'd better let Bessie out again and get another drink. Half an hour later she returned to her book. She knew it was an indulgence to spend a whole morning reading – but when had she last done so? She couldn't remember. Anyway, she was fascinated to find these important women in Christian history. She read on, about Catherine of Siena who had served God during the Black Death, as well as trying to persuade the Pope to go on a crusade! She was outspokenly critical of the luxurious life Pope Gregory XI lived in Avignon under the protection of the French monarchy, and did her utmost to persuade him to move back to Rome.

Martin Luther's wife, Katherina von Bora, reminded her a bit of Susannah Wesley, John Wesley's mother, although Katherina had previously been a nun. Even though she lived in a silent monastery she had somehow heard about the Reformation, and along with ten others from her convent had escaped inside empty herring barrels! Luther's role in this is unclear, but he found himself with responsibility for these ex-nuns. The other ten were soon married, but Katherina refused the man who was recommended to her, and audaciously sent word to Luther that a certain member of his staff would be acceptable, or even Luther himself. They were married in June 1525 and subsequently had six children. She offered hospitality to hundreds of people who came to visit her husband.

The Reformation was a mixed blessing to women. On the positive side it gave dignity and spirituality to marriage. It reaffirmed the roles of wives and mothers, but excluded them from other forms of Christian service. By continuing the tradition of male clergy and removing religious orders, it deprived protestant women of one of the chief ways in which previous generations of women had served God. Many had found considerable freedom to use their spiritual gifts in the life and work of the convents, but the Reformation put nothing comparable in their place for protestant women.

Some strong characters, like Susannah Wesley, made their mark on history in the years following the Reformation, but often they had the opportunity only because of their husband. Susannah had 19 children, and set up a system of educating them. Her husband, Samuel, was the Rector of Epworth. When he was away in London, she held a meeting in the rectory on Sunday evenings, at first for her children and the household servants. When other local people started to join the gathering, Samuel wrote telling her to stop. He gave three reasons, one of which was that she was a woman. She replied to all three points, her response to his argument that she shouldn't do it because she was a woman being:

> . . . as I am a woman so I am also a mistress of a large family. And though the superior charge of souls contained in it lies upon you, as the head of the family, and as their minister, yet in your absence I cannot but look

upon every soul you leave under my care as a talent
committed to me under a trust by the great Lord of all
the families of heaven and earth.

She continued the meetings, and it is said that they
were a key element in encouraging her son John to
preach outside churches, as well as encouraging lay
people to preach during the revival of the early eigh-
teenth century which he and his brother Charles led.
John Wesley did not like women preaching initially,
but he did not have enough male preachers, and people thronged to the midweek classes to hear the
women. He told them to give short words, broken up
with praying and singing and with no preaching, but
the people were so insistent that in the end he capitu-
lated. He justified his decision from Scripture, recognizing that God had done something extraordinary
among the Weslyans, and saw the use of women as
part of God's extraordinary measures for an extraordinary situation. As a result, early Methodists allowed lay people, including women, to take on
leadership roles which were unknown in other
churches (although in 1835 or thereabouts, when the
Methodist Church was trying to regain respectabil-
ity in Anglican eyes, they banned women from
preaching, though some groups protested and broke
away).

What was happening overtly among the Methodists, Joanna discovered, had also happened, though
more quietly, elsewhere:

Throughout the 18th Century women were seen as being more dependent on the comforts and consolations

of religion than men were. As the century wore on there was an increasing emphasis on the unique, albeit carefully circumscribed, superior moral and religious qualities of women.[5]

Women really came into their own again with the emergence of many missionary movements in the 1800s. The Society for Promoting Female Education in the East was founded in England in 1834 to assist single women whom the Lord called to go overseas as teachers to reach local girls and their mothers. It was probably the first such society in the UK and certainly earlier than the North American Women's Societies. In many countries it was impossible for men to speak to women. Moravian wives went overseas with their husbands from the mid-eighteenth century, but for several decades most missionary societies only sent single women if they could join other relatives. As a child, Joanna had been an avid reader and had raided her mother's bookshelf. She recognized some of the names she read about now, such as Mary Slessor, who spent forty years as one of the first missionaries to inland Nigeria, or Ida Scudder, who founded the great medical school and hospital at Vellore in India. She was amazed to find that in the second half of the nineteenth century there were missionary societies which not only had women missionaries, but which were led and administered by women and supported by donations from women. She remembered her mother's series of books by or about Isobel Kuhn, who with her husband spent twenty years as a missionary to the Lisu tribe of south-west China. They'd had to leave when the communists took over China in 1950, and the stories had been current events when her mother bought the books.[6]

There were women in Britain and America too, especially in Victorian times, whose Christian faith drove them to tackle the social evils of the day. People like Annie Macpherson, who worked among the children who made matchboxes in Liverpool, or Agnes Jones, who introduced training schemes into the workhouses and laid the foundation for the development of social work training. Josephine Butler had fought hard to prevent an Act of Parliament which would have allowed child prostitution, while Elizabeth Fry had changed the world of women's prisons. At the same time, there were women working against considerable opposition so that girls could have the opportunity of secondary education. Joanna hadn't realized that if she'd been born a hundred years earlier she might, if she was lucky, have had a few years of schooling so she could read and write, but that would probably have been the end of her education.

Joanna was getting tired. She put the book down and lay back with her eyes closed. She must find time to read the rest of it soon, but for now she had enough to think about. Women had always played a role in the church. Perhaps not very many of them, and it had been extraordinarily difficult for some of them. But people who really wanted to serve God had always found a way of doing so, sometimes within the church and sometimes despite it! So, what was new? And, perhaps more importantly, what should she do?

FOR FURTHER THOUGHT

1 Joanna had become interested in the role of women in the church and wanted to find out more. Is there anything about church life, past, present or future, which particularly interests you? What could you do to find out more – buy a book from a local Christian bookshop, search the Internet, ask others at church, join an evening class?

2 Is there one particular person, from history or in your own life, who especially inspires and encourages you? What is it about his or her life which challenges you? Could you do more yourself to become such a role model or example for others?

Notes

1 The main sources for this chapter are: Lutz, Lorry, *Women as Risk-Takers for God* (Carlisle: WEF in association with Paternoster, 1997), ch. 1. Byrne, Eileen, 'Women's Creative Role in the Church', *Zadok Paper*, Series 1, Paper S57 (Australia: Zadok Institute, 1992). Neil, Stephen, *The Pelican History of the Church: A History of Christian Missions* (London: Penguin, 1986 ed.). The early English history comes from Bede, *Ecclesiastical History of the English People*, D.H. Farmer (ed.), Sherley-Price, Leo (trans.) (London: Penguin, 1990 revised ed.), pp. 243–7. Additional material, Valerie Griffiths.

2 Bede, *Ecclesiastical History*, pp. 243–7.

3 Farmer, D.H. (ed.), *The Age of Bede*, J.F. Webb (trans.) (London: Penguin, 1988 revised edition) pp. 15–6.

4   Petroff, Elizabeth Alvilda, 'The Mystics', *Christian History*, No.2, 1991, quoted in Lutz, *Women as Risk-Takers for God*, p. 10.

5   Gill, Sean, *Women and the Church of England*, (London: SPCK, 1994), p. 11.

6   Kuhn, Isobel, *By Searching* (1957), *In the Arena* (1959), *Ascent to the Tribes* (1956), *Stones of Fire* (1960), *Nests Above the Abyss* (1947) and *Green Leaf in Drought* (1957); Canfield, Caroline, *One Vision Only* (1959). All published by CIM (China Inland Mission), now OMF (Overseas Missionary Fellowship).

5

What Can I Do?

It was always such a rush to get dinner ready. Joanna
had to leave work right on time and dash to collect
Andrew from whatever after-school activity he was
doing that particular night – football training, chess,
music lesson. Sometimes Louise was with him, but
usually she was playing with a friend and Joanna
was very grateful to the mothers who gladly took her
daughter home after school one day a week and kept
an eye on her until after work. Matthew, at 13, was
adamant that he was old enough to be left on his own
for an hour each day, though sometimes the kitchen
looked as though he'd brought an army home with
him to raid the fridge. Saturday was the only day she
could cook the evening meal at leisure, and they
could all sit down and eat together at whatever time
it was ready.

Ever since she'd read that book about women in
church history, Joanna had been thinking and praying about whether she should do more for the
church. They'd been there well over a year, and at
last she was beginning to make real friends. But deep
inside she wanted more than that. She didn't want

going to church to become just a habit. Those women she'd read about had each seen a worthwhile job that needed to be done, and done it for God. For many of them there had been a 'calling', a sense of vocation to their task, but others had just responded to the need they'd seen and taken the next logical step. Either way, they'd made their mark on Christian history. She wasn't wanting to become well known, but the satisfaction of having served God in some way would help her Christian faith to be more at the core of her life. Sometimes these days it felt as if going to church was just one more of the many leisure activities the family were involved in.

The other day while she was window shopping in the high street during her lunch break, she'd decided she wasn't going to wait for someone to ask her, but would explore what possibilities there were. The vicar had been really surprised when she phoned him. He told her he didn't very often have people offer to take on jobs in the church! He asked her what she felt her gifts were, which had rather floored her. She muttered that she didn't really know, but he asked her what she'd done before, in their last church, or when she was a student. She quickly admitted to never wanting to run a crèche again! Then she remembered that at college she'd thoroughly enjoyed helping to lead a student bible study group. They talked for a while, and then he asked her whether Stephen wanted a job at church too! She couldn't answer, so he suggested she get back to him in a couple of weeks when he'd had time to think about what she might be most suitable for, and she'd had time to talk to Stephen.

She raised the subject at dinner on Saturday. They sometimes had a sort of family council over Saturday dinner, so when Stephen said, 'Anyone got anything they want us to discuss tonight?', she leaped in before one of the children could raise the regular questions about pocket money, or use of the phone, or where they should go for their next holiday.

'Yes, I have!' she declared. 'I've been wondering about doing something at church.'

'What – stand on your head in the middle of the sermon?' Matthew responded, at which Andrew sniggered and Louise immediately snapped back,

'Don't be so stupid. Boys!'

She was grateful when Stephen tried to start the conversation again by asking what she had in mind. She wasn't sure, she told him, but then started to explain how this had come about. She told them about the book she'd read, and how God had used women throughout church history. She reminded them of Whitby, and Hilda, and briefly told the stories of some of the women. Stephen was looking at her with a puzzled expression. He couldn't quite see the relevance of this, so he tried another tack. Why did she want to 'do something'? Fumbling with the words at first she began to talk about the things that had been going through her mind in the past few months: about God having done so much for her that she wanted to do something for Him as a thank you, not wanting to be a spectator at church but be part of the action, the feeling she had that the more she put in the more she'd get back and discovering through her job that she had skills which she wanted to use not only to earn money but also to serve God. The more

she talked, the more confident she felt that this was
the right thing to do, and that somehow God was
pleased with her.

They talked on for quite a long time. Gradually
the children drifted away to watch television or play
computer games, but she and Stephen had one of the
best discussions they'd had for ages. He admitted to
having also wondered whether he could do more as
a Christian. His job was a good one, but there must
be more to life than going to work, coming home,
eating and sleeping. By the middle of the evening
they'd agreed that they should go and see the vicar
together and leave it with him as to whether they
took on a joint job or each did something separately.

*   *   *   *   *

We have already looked in chapter one at why people, especially women, go to church. It is a slightly
different question to consider what they get out of
going. The reason why you get out of bed and into
church on a Sunday is not quite the same as the
thoughts you might have after church about the benefits of having been there, although there is some
overlap.

What women 'get out' of church

Women I talked to gave a variety of answers to this
question:

- Contact with others in the church
- Encouragement, both personally and spiritually

- Fellowship
- Friends not met elsewhere
- Meet with and focus on God
- Oasis in a busy life
- Opportunity to give as well as receive
- Perspective on life
- Satisfaction in using gifts
- Serving God
- Spiritual challenge
- Spiritual food

You can see immediately that just like the earlier list of the reasons for going to church, these are a mixture of what might be termed spiritual and practical factors. Which ones do you identify with? Suppose you wrote a list when you returned from church, headed 'It was good to be in church today because . . .' – what would you put on it?

Several of the above answers are to do with relationships, whether with God or with other people. As we've already seen, relationships are a key part of church life for women. However, relationships can be as much about meeting your needs as about the other person's. This list goes beyond that and shows that an important part of churchgoing for many women is the opportunity to serve God.

Reasons for serving God

Women want church to be not only about receiving spiritual or practical support and encouragement, but also about giving it. The women in the research

groups saw this as giving something back to the
church. Why did they want to do that? For the kind
of reasons that had set Joanna thinking.

Gratitude

The Christian life is a two-way relationship with
God. People who have come to a personal, day by
day faith in God want to find ways of thanking him.
It may be an individual thing, perhaps through
prayer. But many people want to find a public expression for their gratitude. One woman commented, 'The service we give to God is the rent we
pay for the room on earth.' It isn't that we have to
serve God, but that we want to.

There is also gratitude to people. This may mean,
for example, being willing to teach in Sunday School
partly because you had a brilliant Sunday School
teacher as a child. The memory of that teacher has
lived on, and one way to say thank you is to pass on
to the next generation what you learned from the
previous one.

Friendship

Friendship is also two-way, and having found
friends in church it is natural to express those friendships by wanting to do things with and for one's
friends. One way of getting to know people is by
working with them. For many women it doesn't really matter what the job is, but who they do it with.

Spending time working together is a good way to find out much more about a person than a brief conversation on the way out of church or over coffee in the hall. It may lead to opportunities to encourage and help each other spiritually, and perhaps to pray together or for one another.

Showing love

God has shown his love for us in Jesus Christ, and he expects us to show that love to others. This is a strong motivating factor for some people. Church is about people, and for some it is very important to contribute what they can, in order to show their love for the other members of the congregation. They do this in ways that are appropriate to their gifts and skills, which don't have to be obvious or upfront. One person may make sure they speak to visitors to the church, someone else visits people who are ill, and another takes their turn on the crèche rota.

Using gifts

We all have gifts, and finding appropriate ways to use them seems to be an important part of reaching that sense of belonging we discussed earlier. When the interviewees were specifically asked what gifts they had, everyone knew they had several. The list of gifts compiled from the various groups is very varied and here they are grouped together, with examples of what each involves.

Gifts used in the church

Caring for people	Visiting, welcoming
Counselling	Formally or informally
Creativity	Banner making, flower arranging, writing magazine, producing newsletter
Hospitality	Providing meals at home or church
Leadership	Small groups, PCC member or deacon
Music and/ or drama	Choir, worship group, special events
Organisation	Writing and distributing notices, arranging events
Outreach/evangelism	Planning or taking part
Practical tasks	Tea making, counting and banking offerings, cleaning
Praying for others	Prayer chain, during or after services
Preaching	
Providing resources	Giving money, food
Teaching	Sunday School, small groups

There are others ways in which gifts can be used, for example youth work, contact with other churches or Christian agencies, or missionary support.

Using your gifts, however, assumes that you know what your gifts are! If you are unsure there are various ways of finding out. Asking at your local Christian bookshop for a book on gifts is one way.

Another is to ask people who know you well what they think your gifts are. Some churches include a session on discovering your gifts in courses such as preparation for confirmation, baptism or church membership. Another way can be to use a simple questionnaire to help identify what gifts you have subconsciously been using. Some Christian teaching separates spiritual gifts, as listed in various places in the Bible, from natural gifts that we may have been born with, or learned in different ways. Here's a very practical questionnaire which doesn't distinguish whether the gifts are spiritual or practical.[1]

Divide your life into intervals of roughly five years, since you started school. For each period write down one thing you did of which, looking back now, you are proud and then number them. If you want to list two things while you were at school and three when you were in your twenties, that's fine. What is important is that you choose things which cover the entire span of your life. Then look at the grid below. The numbers along the top correspond with the achievement at each period of your life. Tick in the grid those characteristics which contributed to your achievements each time they occur. When you've gone through the grid for each achievement, add up the number of ticks in each row. Which rows have the highest numbers of ticks? There may be three or four, or perhaps more. The results show your key skills, and you may find one or two surprises among them.

Table of skills											
Skill	1	2	3	4	5	6	7	8	9	10	Total
Analysis											
Artistic ability											
Budget formation											
Control (people or things)											
Co-ordination											
Creativity											
Design ability											
Detailed work											
Economy											
Energy or drive											
Follow through											
Foresight											
Human relations											
Ideas											
Imagination											
Individualism											
Initiative											
Inventiveness											
Leadership											
Liaison											
Management											
Mechanical											
Memorisation											
Negotiation											
Numerical ability											

| *Table of skills* (continued) | | | | | | | | | | |
Skill	1	2	3	4	5	6	7	8	9	10	Total
Observation											
Organisation											
Outdoors/ travel											
Ownership (things)											
People/ personnel											
Perceptiveness											
Perseverance											
Persuasiveness											
Planning											
Policy making											
Practical ability											
Problem solving											
Production											
Programming											
Promotion											
Research											
Selling											
Service given											
Showmanship											
Speaking											
Systems/ procedures											
Training											
Trouble shooting											
Words											
Writing											

What kinds of gifts are women most comfortable exercising?

The gifts a woman may use in church vary enormously, according to her personality, experience and training, as well as the needs and opportunities of her church. Some women who don't go out to work, either because they have chosen not to, or because they are retired, may be in a position to give time to the church in a way that others cannot, or which they couldn't earlier in their lives. They may be the regular helpers at a luncheon club, be available to tourists visiting a well-known building, take communion to those unable to attend church or help to hold services in old people's homes. It would seem that for such women, especially the older ones, it often doesn't matter what they do, they are simply glad of the opportunity to be involved. However, the specific use of women's gifts can be a touchy subject, and quite a few strong points were made in the various groups!

Discussion in the groups centred around four kinds of gifts which these women, at least, felt comfortable using.

Practical gifts

Disparaging remarks are sometimes made about women 'only being allowed to do the flowers and make tea'. But some women enjoy doing the flowers, or making tea, and they're good at it! There is certainly a big difference between going into a church where the flowers are beautifully arranged, and one where they seem to have been thrust into the vase in such a way that you almost feel sorry for the flowers. Any problems don't lie in the task, but rather when women who simply aren't good at flower arranging or making tea, or who don't enjoy it, are expected to take on these jobs simply because they are women.

Caring roles

This is a practical expression of the sense of belonging and shows an identity with, and commitment to, the community which is the local church. This needs to be shown in practical ways. It may be similar to practical concern for one's neighbours, such as noticing whether someone is not in church when you would expect them to be and phoning to check they are OK, or visiting members of the church who are in hospital or residential homes.

In other churches there may be specific care roles available. For example my current local church runs a Disabled Christians Fellowship, and the monthly meetings involve a considerable number of people from the church in tasks like collecting people and taking them home, as well as being present during the afternoon to provide whatever help anyone needs. Other churches have linked up with secular caring groups in their community to offer help with tasks like shopping or simple household repairs for those who are unable to do such things for themselves.

Leadership

Much has been written and said in recent years about whether or not women should be ordained. But many women who have no interest in being ordained are already exercising leadership in a wide variety of ways. This may be in an obvious role, such as in a youth group or home group. However, women with no specific leadership role may nevertheless be exercising a form of leadership without realizing it. This was pursued in the research groups by asking, 'Do you feel spiritually responsible for anyone in your church?' The answers were very varied, and showed that you don't have to be in an official position to take responsibility for others and thus in some sense provide leadership for them.

People for whom spiritual responsibility is felt

    Alpha course participants
    Anyone who is sick or having problems
    Children – those taught and their own
    Choirs
    Ecumenical groups e.g. Lent groups
    Friends brought to church
    Home group members
    Personal friends
    Prayer partners
    'Shut-ins' to whom they take home communion

Exercising this sense of spiritual responsibility is in effect a form of leadership and one which is open to anyone, whatever the opportunities for the more obvious leadership roles.

Evangelism and mission

Most churches have some form of outreach into the local community or even further afield. The terms used for it vary. It's often called evangelism in evangelical churches, but the women in the research groups who were not from evangelical churches were involved in similar kinds of mission. Asking what kind of evangelism they were involved in brought us straight back to relationships! Some were involved in organized activities, such as Alpha courses, special events arranged by the church, visiting church contacts, or children's activities such as weekly clubs at school or church, or holiday clubs. However, for virtually all of them, evangelism was primarily about talking to friends when the subject of faith or church came up, praying for neighbours and friends who had no Christian faith, and simply living out their faith at all times. They were happier talking to people one-to-one or sharing in a small group, rather than getting involved in big events.

Bringing a friend to church was definitely seen as evangelism, and most of those interviewed had invited someone to church within the past year – although not all of those invited had actually come. The majority of the women in the groups had brought a friend to church, and some were now regular members of the congregation, while others were still exploring the Christian faith through groups such as Alpha, Emmaus or Just Looking.

At a conference on church planting, one discussion group looked specifically at the role of women in church planting, with some interesting conclusions:[2]

Where men are leading, they build a network church of people with similar interests drawn from a wide area: where women are leading they build a neighbourhood church.

Many women bring female friends to church, then those friends bring men.

Women tend to be more personal in their contacts.

FACT BOX

One of the biggest churches in the UK is Kensington Temple (London City Church) in west London. Kensington Temple are involved in church planting in a massive way, and 75% of their church planting groups are (or were) composed of women.

Churches need to recognize that women can be good personal evangelists, and encourage them to 'gossip the gospel', as someone once put it!

*   *   *   *   *

Why do some women not use their gifts?

As Joanna and Stephen talked, they shared with one another the kind of roles they felt might suit them. Stephen was surprised when Joanna said she didn't feel comfortable in a leadership role.

'But you're always having to make decisions, both at home and at work,' he responded. 'And you helped lead a bible study group at college. You once led a small group at the Christian Union when I was there, and I thought you did it very well. It's one of the first times I remember noticing you!'

'But I haven't done anything like that since,' replied Joanna.

Stephen couldn't see what that had to do with it. He had recently been on an interview panel for a new appointment to his office where the personnel officer had remarked that a man would apply for a job if he could do 75% of what was in the job description, while a woman wouldn't apply because of the 25% she couldn't do. He'd also heard about a survey investigating why four times as many men as women applied for research grants.[3] He wondered if Joanna was falling into the same way of thinking.

Joanna's response was to go and find a magazine article she'd kept, because it rang bells with her feelings about herself. She read out one paragraph to Stephen, which was attempting to answer the question: 'What is the one thing that you feel really prevents women experiencing freedom in Christ?' The reply was:

I would say there are two things: identity and self-image. Despite the fact that women have been pushed forward and given a more prominent role in society, I still think they suffer from negative self-image. There are so many negative influences that affect women in that way. Also some women carry around with them a whole range of negative emotions from past hurts and disappointments. This often leads to women being hindered in how they can function and express themselves in the Church.[4]

* * * * *

Time and again women told me about their own struggles, or those of people known well to them. They fell into several groups.

Uncertainty about themselves

In the research it was frequently found that one of the reasons women don't do more in church is because they don't think that they can. One interviewee stated that part of the reason why women don't take on key roles in the church is

> because of their attitude of "I can't do it." They don't actually believe in themselves; they don't realize who they are in Christ.

Another commented,

> Men are amazingly confident about what they can do, even if they are entirely inadequate for the job. Women are more tentative about what they can offer and often need the encouragement of others to get started.

However, this was clearly felt much more strongly by older women. In one group a woman in her twenties found it hard to believe that anyone still thought that way! It seems that there are two related issues – a woman's self-image and her identity as a Christian believer. If she has problems with either, she will struggle to use her gifts in the service of God. If she has problems with both, she probably will not use her gifts at all, however much she is encouraged.

They think their gifts aren't acceptable

Some women feel that their gifts will not be welcome in the church because they aren't what the church wants or needs. This may be because they think the church is a man's world, or because they have experienced what is or feels like discrimination because they are women. This is a thorny issue which we'll look at in more depth later. In this chapter we are dealing with women's attitudes and responsibilities rather than those of the churches. It isn't always easy to separate the two, but some women will blame the church for not allowing them to use their gifts when actually they could, if they had the confidence.

The church is a community, a family, a body of believers, and as such needs the kind of gifts women are often comfortable to exercise.

> The chief New Testament metaphors for being a Christian are not drawn from male-dominated activities such as warfare, politics, international trade, or even high art. They are mainly metaphors concerned with giving birth (witnessing so that others can be 'born again'), nurturing (patiently discipling others), caring for the body (of interdependent believers), and taking the lower status of a servant – all activities taken as the more 'natural domain of women!'[5]

Many women could do more to serve God if they were prepared to contribute the gifts they have. Are you one of those who is unwilling to use her gifts? Why? Would you like to change that?

A few women I talked to were honest about their
struggles in this area, but also shared practical steps
they'd taken about it. One had attended one of the
assertiveness courses which seem to be all the rage
these days! However, most help had come through
sharing concerns with a close friend or an older
woman in the church, and praying about them. This
helped a woman see God's perspective on her gifts,
rather than her own. If a poor view of oneself
stemmed from hurtful childhood experiences, then
facing up to them meant seeking help, perhaps
through reading a good Christian or secular book on
the subject, or through going for counselling.
Working through such painful issues and coming
out the other side had greatly affected these
women's lives in a wide range of ways, including
whether they had the courage to use their gifts.

Practical pressures

Full-time employment can make a regular commitment to church very difficult. To get in from work at
perhaps 6.30 p.m., then prepare a meal, deal with
any family crises, make sure Matthew is doing his
homework, and be out again to help lead a church
youth club at 7.30 p.m. takes a lot of organizing, and
a lot of energy. Not everyone has it!

One of the results of more women working outside the home is that some of the events and forms of
outreach for women that were popular 15 or 20 years
ago are no longer realistic in many churches. So outreach coffee mornings or women's luncheons may

still work in some places, but most churches and groups which used to organize such events have had to develop other activities which fit in with women's lives today.[6]

Mothers at home with small children face a different set of pressures. As one explained, 'The expectation is that as a teacher and a mother I will teach Sunday School. But I'm with children all week, so I don't want to be with them in Sunday School as well.' Someone else remarked, 'Just because I have my own children doesn't mean I enjoy teaching them.' Remember, Joanna was determined not to run the crèche again!

Older women have been the backbone of many Sunday Schools. They've seen generations of children go through their classes. These days many of them find it increasingly difficult to relate to the teaching styles that children are used to at school. Gone seem to be the days when children would sit quietly and listen to a story for 10 or 15 minutes – although they seem to manage it in 'story times' at local libraries! They also think in different ways. Older children and teenagers have been dubbed 'mosaics'[7] because they gather all sort of pieces of information from a wide range of sources and create their own picture, rather than thinking in linear logic as their grandparents were taught to.[8] This can mean that older people feel their gifts are no longer appropriate or welcome, especially in youth and children's work. Finding out how children learn these days can enable older people to continue to teach children and young people effectively, and often generates spin-offs in other ways such as realizing why children's TV programmes are so different from 20 or 30 years ago.

Family demands

Many husbands don't share their wife's faith, which can have the negative effect that if a husband is not fully involved, he doesn't see why his wife should be. For others there are the demands of being a full-time carer. Arranging care for an elderly relative who can't be left alone may be unrealistic, and caring is hard work leaving many carers with little energy for other activities.

Conclusion

In modern society, it's not hard to feel discouraged; we only have to look at the pressures in the home, the workplace, on our children – especially our teenagers – and the frequent feelings of hopelessness within our nation. But faith can never merely observe; we have to act and believe in the possibility of change. I'm not saying we can change the world, but we can change somebody's world – we can do something.[9]

Maybe you could do more than you're doing now. If so, how about taking a few minutes to think and pray about what steps you need to take to express your Christian faith in practical ways, and to use your gifts for the service of God and your local church or neighbourhood.

FOR FURTHER THOUGHT

1 Joanna wasn't sure what her gifts were, or how she wanted to use them. Do you know what your gifts are? Do you have any gifts which you are not using in your church, but which you could be?

2 Do you identify with any of the reasons why some women do not use their gifts? Could you take any practical steps to make some changes?

3 'We can change somebody's world – we can do something.' What 'something' are you doing as part of your Christian life? Perhaps you could help and encourage someone else to use her gifts e.g. by mentoring a younger person who is not confident enough to take on a role on her own, but who could do it with your support.

Notes

1 Brierley, Peter, *Vision Building* (London: Christian Research, 1994 reprint), p.116.
2 *Church Growth Digest*, Vol. 15, No. 2, p. 11.
3 Reported in *Wellcome News*, Q3 98, p. 4.
4 Interview with Amanda Dye in *Woman Alive*, March 1999.
5 Leeuwen, Mary Stewart van, *Gender and Grace* (Nottingham: IVP, 1990) quoted in 'What Men can Learn from Women (and Jesus) about Leadership', Valdez, Edna and Wright, Kim, *Together* magazine, Oct.-Dec. 1992, p. 15.
6 Organizations such as Christian Viewpoint and Women Reaching Women have faced such issues.

7 Brierley, Peter, *The Tide is Running Out* (London: Christian Research, 2000), p.106

8 The difficulty older people have in teaching Sunday School became very clear through a research project undertaken by Christian Research on behalf of Scripture Union.

9 Diane Parsons in 'Changing the Face of Society', *Care for the Family* magazine, Spring 2000, p.2.

6

What Women Believe

'Chris, are you busy on Wednesday evening? Would you be willing to come round and be with the kids while Stephen and I go out? We're going to see the vicar to talk about whether there's anything we can do in the church. We'll only be gone an hour or so. Matthew thinks he's old enough to look after them – but he gets a lot of homework these days and once he gets stuck into that with his music on full volume, he probably wouldn't notice if the house burned down, and certainly not if Andrew and Louise had a fight or if Bessie was desperate to be let out . . .

'. . . You are? Oh, that's great! Would you like to come early and have dinner with us all . . .?

'. . . Lovely. We'll look forward to seeing you about half-past six then. Have a good week. Bye.'

As she put the phone down, Joanna breathed a thankful prayer for her deepening friendship with Chris. They had so much in common, and recently had started praying together.

A sudden blast of pop music changed the atmosphere instantly. Could Matthew really be a teenager? It hardly seemed any time since she'd brought home that bundle of new life from the hospital. The music blaring from his bedroom reminded her that he was developing his own likes and dislikes, and that it would not be many years before he flew the nest. Life was changing. The children didn't need her quite as much now: that had been quite clear from the way they'd happily adjusted to her working full-time. She somehow felt that she had a bit more energy to put into life outside the home and work.

Since that Saturday evening a couple of weeks ago, Joanna and Stephen had talked quite a bit about what they could do in the church. Stephen was inclined to feel that it would be logical for him to fit in where he could use his gifts and skills, while Joanna approached the decision more by praying that God would guide them. They'd discussed whether to offer to lead a home group; after all, they'd done that in their last church. Stephen wasn't as keen as Joanna. Work often took him away from home for a day or two and he really had no control over when he had to go. He felt that if he was going to take on a church responsibility he wanted to do it properly, and not have to keep saying he couldn't be there – again.

One of the key things they discussed at length was whether it was important to do something together. Stephen would have preferred to, but Joanna felt she'd like to explore her gifts and abilities on her own, without her husband. That debate went on for several days! Stephen had very mixed feelings about it. Sometimes he felt quite miffed that Joanna wanted to be independent, and at other times he was pleased that she wanted to find her own feet in the church. Joanna had a sense of anticipation, of wanting to set out on her own and see what she could achieve. She somehow felt she was growing spiritually. Her thinking and reading over the past few months had stimulated her into realizing that she didn't need to sit back and let everything come to her. She could play an active part in the church, and put back into church life some of what she had received.

A comment from Matthew had helped them to decide. He came in from the youth group excited and bubbling to tell them something. There was a youth football league in the town, and they'd been discussing whether to get together a team for the next season, which was starting very soon. If they were to go for it, they had to decide in the next few days. The biggest problem was that they had to have an adult as their coach or manager – a person who could organize their fixtures and be a contact point. Another problem was that there weren't enough parents willing to drive them to matches.

To Matthew the answer was obvious: 'Dad, you're wanting to do something in the church. What could be better? You're always at home at weekends and you never do much other than a bit of gardening. You used to play football for your university and you're a manager at work, so you must be able to coach and organize us. And we've got a car. You could do it. I've already told the group you will. The meeting to sort it all out is after church on Sunday evening. You will do it, won't you Dad? And of course, you'd have to come to the youth club on Friday night so you get to know us all.'

Stephen was initially taken aback, but the more they talked, the more he warmed to the idea. Joanna definitely didn't want to help lead a football team, and anyway, if her husband and older son were going to be out a fair bit at the weekends, she'd need to be around for Andrew and Louise. By Sunday evening Stephen had agreed to go to the meeting, and Joanna knew he'd say yes. That left her free to take on an independent role in the church, but she still wasn't sure what. Hopefully the vicar would have some helpful suggestions, though deep down she had a growing sense that she would like to take on some kind of leadership role.

*   *   *   *   *

Women's beliefs

It is commonly accepted that women are more religious than men. There is much debate about why women see religion differently, but there is no doubt that they do. Evidence of this includes the fact that more women than men go to church (we saw that in chapter two). Two-thirds of the fall in churchgoing in England in the 1980s was due to men dropping out, which has major implications for men, but looking at how men relate to church must be the subject of another research project.[1] Unfortunately the 1998 English Church Attendance Survey didn't ask about gender, so we don't know statistically whether men have continued to drop out of church in greater numbers than women, but most anecdotal evidence suggests the trend has continued.

FACT BOX

The following theories have been proposed to account for the religious differences between men and women.[2]

Sex roles

> *Basic idea* – men and women are brought up with distinct ideals and values
>
> *Religious effect* – women are gentler, and learn nurturing skills and interpersonal values which fit easily into a religious lifestyle

Structural, location

> *Basic idea* – a mother's role is family centred, a father's economic
>
> *Religious effect* – religion emphasizes the importance of family. Mothers also carry more responsibility for passing on moral values to their children, one of the main sources for which is religion

Gender orientation

> *Basic idea* – feminine and masculine personalities are different
>
> *Religious effect* – people with a more feminine personality (including some men) are more comfortable with religion

Psychological

> *Basic idea* – God is portrayed as a father
>
> *Religious effect* – girls have a different relationship with their father from boys and more easily transfer their love from their father to God

Personality

> *Basic idea* – some of the differences between males and females are indirectly related to religion
>
> *Religious effect* – women, for example, feel more guilt than men and are thus more responsive to religion which offers a mechanism for coping with guilt.

However, 'being religious' is much more than simple attendance at a place of worship. It involves what you believe, and how you put it into practice in your life. And it's in this sense that women are seen to be more religious than men.

Let's look briefly at some of the beliefs and behaviour which have been measured and show that women are more religious than men.

Table 1: *Gender differences in religious belief, Britain*[3]

Belief in:	Females %	Males %	Difference %
Heaven	69	50	+19
Souls	76	58	+18
Life after death	57	39	+18
God	84	67	+17
The devil	42	32	+10
Hell	35	27	+ 8
Sin	72	66	+ 6
No belief in God	9	16	− 7

More women than men believe in all the items in this list. The *Soul of Britain* survey for the BBC, published in the summer of 2000, showed a much lower overall percentage of people believing in God, and doubtless other levels of belief have dropped too.[4] Unfortunately the survey results were not available by gender when this book was written, although hopefully they may be eventually.

One of the core values of the Christian faith is the importance of the Bible as the foundation for our beliefs. In another survey,[5] women showed a more positive attitude towards the Bible (on a scale of 1–10, where 10 is positive, men scored 6.6 and women 7.0). They found God to be more important in their lives than men (men scored 5.1 on the same scale, women 6.4) and viewed the church more favourably (men 5.1, women 6.4). More women thought that the church met people's spiritual needs (men 16%, women 25%) – though back in 1983 when this survey was done, those interviewed represented only a small proportion of the whole population!

The survey which identified the issues to study in the present research asked a number of questions about various aspects of belief and behaviour. One of the results it showed was that men and women read the Bible for different reasons.

Women read the Bible more than men to:

- Seek guidance and inspiration
- Find comfort in times of illness, crisis or loneliness
- Teach their children Christianity.

Men read the Bible more than women to:

- Study and learn about God
- Follow up references given in church or bible study notes.

It is immediately obvious that women read the Bible because of the help and support it can give them, while men read it to learn about their faith. Women's reasons could be said to be emotional, and the men's more intellectual. This was why Joanna was more inclined to pray for guidance, and perhaps look to the Bible to find it, while Stephen expected a logical solution to their offer to take on a job in the church.

This is borne out by answers to a question about how people's lives are influenced by the Bible. Women only came out more strongly than men in one way – the Bible influenced their daily Christian lives, which could be understood to mean that it underlies much of their day-to-day behaviour. However, the ways in which men came out as being more strongly influenced by the Bible than women were much more to do with how they think: their knowledge and understanding of God, attitudes to the poor and disadvantaged and also to material possessions, wealth and their moral conduct.

Perhaps this underlies a marvellous statement by David Yonggi Cho, leader of the biggest churches in the world in Seoul, Korea. He is reported to have said:

> If you want to build an organisation, use men. If you want to build the church, use women.[6]

Men have proved themselves over the centuries more than capable of organizing the church and running it structurally – sometimes too well, some women think, because it is done in a very masculine way which has in itself excluded women before any considerations of theology are taken into account. However, a careful reading of church history shows that women have always been the backbone of day-to-day church life at a local level, and the glue which holds it together.[7]

A set of questions in the same survey asked people how strongly they believed in six statements which could be considered central to the Christian faith, such as, 'I believe in God the Father who created the world,' and 'I believe that Jesus Christ died for the sin of the world.' With every statement and in almost every church women were much more likely than men to say they believed without question. This suggests that women are much less inclined than men to question what they believe. Now, whether that is a good thing or a bad thing is a big debate, but it certainly underlines the fact that we approach our faith in a different way to men!

This different approach to faith has various practical applications. One example comes from the area of community development in poorer nations

> One of the major discoveries in the field of community development during the last 10 years is the critical importance of women to the development process . . . Empowering women is one of the keys to transforming the larger community . . . If the education and empowerment of women leads to positive social change, might women also be critical to spiritual transformation?[8]

This investigation uncovered a piece of research from the early 1800s in America which drew the following conclusions:

> Women had an image of God that was relational. God was described as father, friend, soul-mate and lover. Men saw God as law-giver, sovereign and king.
>   Women thought of sin in terms of failed or flawed re-

lationships. For men sin meant breaking the laws or rules.

For women, conversion sometimes was a form of liberation from oppressive fathers and husbands; whereas for men conversion sometimes was motivated by a reaction against unjust social rules.

This pattern of gender differences is similar to those we've just looked at. It also is in line with those described in an important book on the subject, *In a Different Voice*, which is often considered to have sparked off many of the recent debates about gender difference.[9] We have to be careful about implying that *difference* between men and women is the same as saying that women are *better*![10] Churchgoing women in Scotland felt a deep concern to 'express our needs, dissatisfactions and hopes not in an angry or aggressive manner towards men, but as partners, as equals in the quest to build up the kingdom of God.'[11]

Men, women and the church

Many women in the church today have grown up in a society which proclaims equality – for men and women, black and white, the able-bodied and the disabled and so on. Some express this as freedom (whether 'freedom from' or 'freedom to') rather than equality.[12] Yet we don't have to look far to realize that such equality or freedom for women is still only an ideal in many respects. Worldwide, women are woefully undervalued. Women represent nearly half of the world's adult population, yet in 1980 they comprised one-third of the official labour force, did two-thirds of all working hours, received one-tenth of the world's income and owned less than one-hundredth of its property.[13]

Many women feel the injustice of this deeply, and many of us find ourselves in some sympathy with the feminist perspective, even though we may not want to embrace it wholeheartedly. That affects our view of society and of the church. We may belong now, or know friends who belong, to a church which embodies Elaine Storkey's description:

> The Church ... wants women in their 'normal', 'proper' roles. It is happiest with women who are supportive and domestic, women who are uncritical and non-threatening, docile, feminine, good followers, hospitable and passive. Most churches are embarrassed with women who feel called to leadership, women who are perceptive and analytical, women who are learned in Scripture and have developed biblical insights.[14]

One aspect of feminist dissatisfaction with the church in general has been with the way its structures have been developed by men with a masculine pattern and continue, by and large, to be run by men. Some have taken issue with gender-related language in the Bible and liturgies. Others have expressed deep reservations about the way the church limits the role of women. A few have even blamed the church for all the ills of society.

FACT BOX

A short guide to varieties of feminist thought[15]

Liberal Feminism
> *Belief* – gender differences are primarily socially determined
> *Emphasizes* – equality of opportunity unhindered by laws or customs related to gender, race or ethnicity

Marxist Feminism
> *Belief* – gender differences are a result of capitalism forcing women into non-productive roles
> *Emphasizes* – equality of opportunity in a classless society

Radical Feminism
> *Belief* – gender differences are created when women are subordinated to men for biological reasons (e.g. women's childbearing and chilrearing burdens)
> *Emphasizes* – equality of opportunity is unlikely except in women-centred alternatives

Socialist Feminism
> *Believes* – gender differences are a result of individual, interpersonal, social and economic factors
> *Emphasizes* – equality of opportunity is possible if society is radically restructured from the economic base up.

Different women are different too!

One of the dangers of the kind of arguments we've looked at in this chapter is to imply that all women think, believe and behave in one way, and all men in another. We all know that life is nowhere near as straightforward as that! Before we end this chapter we need to look briefly at some of the differences between women, using an outline given by Elaine Storkey at a lecture in 1994.[16] She described four kinds of women, and how they relate to the church.

The new woman

Often a young, professional, able, competent woman, she has grown up in a very different gender culture from her mother and especially her grandmother. Freedom for her is the right to make her own decisions with no reference to 'you' – whoever 'you' may be. She is post-feminist, and doesn't challenge the hierarchical nature of society, but just wants to get to the top of it! For most 'new women', Christianity is as outdated as the old buildings it so often worships in. For the few who still attend church, it is a struggle to understand the ethos and find a way to relate faith to the rest of life.

The suffering woman

These women have either opted out of the new woman's rat race, or they never started out in it. They may be single mothers, at the bottom end of the income scale, or abused wives and ex-wives. They may carry deep scars from experiences in childhood or more recent events which they have survived, but only just. These are women to whom the gospel could offer hope where there is none, family to replace those they've lost or never had, and healing for their pain. It rarely gets the chance to do so, because these women feel excluded by the church, are afraid because it seems too full of men in positions of power, and wary of the guilt it seems to lay on them.

The angry woman

This woman is angry, often because she is cynical. She doesn't want simplistic answers to life's deep problems, especially when those 'answers' come to her from an institution that she perceives as either patriarchal (in Western countries) or colonial (in the developing world). At the extreme end of this perspective is the woman who camped out for years at Greenham Common, or took up other issues to protest about. Many of these women have left the church because they are no longer prepared:

> to argue against the inferiority which the church institution imposes on us. This means working to an agenda which has been framed for us; which is not aimed to meet our needs or to utilize our gifts and experience. It leaves us bored, frustrated and hurt.[17]

Other women have remained loyal to the church, yet nevertheless feel that their voice isn't heard, their contribution not valued, and their difference from men deemed to be inferiority. The church needs to listen to these people, and perhaps this book will help it to do so.

The Christian woman

This woman has a strong, firm faith in God, and is still confident in who she is as a believer. She's like Joanna, growing in faith, exploring possibilities and finding opportunities to use her gifts. She may have been, or still be at least in part, a new woman, a suffering woman, or an angry woman, but she is finding help and strength in her Christian commitment and in her local community of believers. I hope you are one of them.

FOR FURTHER THOUGHT

1 Joanna felt she wanted to explore her gifts and abilities, and use them for the benefit of the church. What do you feel you would really like to do in the church, given the opportunity? What is stopping you?

2 Do you recognize yourself, partly or completely, in the new woman, the suffering woman, or the angry woman? In what ways, if any, do you think the church in general or your church in particular undervalues or misunderstands women like you?

Notes

1 In the summer of 2000 Roy McCloughry of the Kingdom Trust was planning such a project.

2 Kay, William K. and Francis, Leslie J., *Drift from the Churches* (Cardiff: University of Wales Press, 1996), ch. 2.

3 McCloughry, Roy, 'Are Men As Religious As Women?', *Christianity*, Oct. 1999.

4 *Soul of Britain*, research undertaken by Gordon Heald of ORB for the BBC, June 2000

5 Harrison, Jan, *Attitudes to Bible, God and Church* (Swindon: Bible Society, 1983).

6 Simson, Wolfgang, *Houses that Change the World: The Return of the House Churches* (Carlisle: Paternoster, 2001), p. 102.

7 'Professor Patrick Collinson divided historical writing on women into two types, the pessimistic and the optimistic, the school which believes that women have been discriminated against by men throughout the ages and sets out to document this oppression, and the other which, while not minimizing the difficulties with which women have had to contend, emphasizes their achievements rather than their failures.' Shiels, W. J. and Wood, Diana (eds.), *Studies in Church History*, Vol.27, published for The Ecclesiastical History Society (Oxford: Basil Blackwell, 1990), introduction p. xix.

8 Myers, Bryant, 'Women and Mission', *MARC Newsletter*, Number 93–3, Sept. 1993. A similar question was posed by Harriet A. Harris in a paper given at the Oxford Conference on Christian Response to Population Issues, reported in *Transformation*, June 1996.

9 Gilligan, Carol, *In a Different Voice*, (Cambridge, Massachusetts: Harvard University Press, 1982).

10 Robbins, Mandy, 'A Different Voice, A Different View', *Review of Religious Research*, Vol. 40, No. 1, Sept. 1998.

11 Hart, Margaret, *To Have A Voice* (Edinburgh: Saint Andrew Press, 1995), p. 4, on behalf of Network of Ecumenical Women in Scotland.

12 Timms, Noel, *Family and Citizenship: Values in Contemporary Britain* (Aldershot: Dartmouth, 1992), p. 41.

13 United Nations, quoted in Hill, Elizabeth, *Gender Inequality* (Australia: Zadok Institute, Zadok/TEAR occasional publication, undated), p. 16.

14 Storkey, Elaine, *What's Right with Feminism?* (London: SPCK, 1985), p. 48.

15 'Feminism and the Church', *Context*, Vol. 5, Issue 2 (MARC Canada, Oct. 1995), p. 4.

16 Storkey, Elaine, *Henry Martyn Lecture 1994* (London: Evangelical Missionary Alliance, 1994).

17 Miles, Rosie, *Not in Our Name: Voices of Women who have left the Church* (Nottingham: Southwell Diocesan Social Responsibility Group, 1994), p. v.

7

You Want To What?!

Rachel was coming for the weekend. Joanna was excited and wanted the whole house to look its best for her old friend. Louise had helped her clear all the bits and pieces off the spare bed, some of which must have been there since they moved! Matthew's reaction was that he wasn't going to clean up his bedroom for anyone, and anyway, why did she need to see his bedroom? Rachel was his mother's friend, not his. Andrew's main concern was whether Stephen would still be able to take him to the school football match on Saturday morning.

Rachel and Joanna had met in their first year at college and, with three other friends, had shared a house for their second and third years. After college they'd met at least once a year, but once they'd each married the visits had gradually become less regular. Rachel had a senior job in a finance company, and hadn't started her family for several years. Her oldest, Samantha – always known as Sam – was a bit younger than Louise, so Joanna had invited her as well. That way, she reasoned, Sam and Louise could play together and she and Rachel might have more time to talk. She deliberately hadn't invited Timothy, who was three.

Their train arrived on time, and Joanna scanned the Friday night crowds which poured off it. There they were. Suddenly Joanna wished she hadn't put on slacks and a baggy sweater after work. She'd forgotten how tall and elegant Rachel was and because she'd come almost straight from work, just pausing to pick up Sam, she was still wearing a smart trouser suit. Briefly Joanna wondered whether the gap between them would be too big to bridge, but that was swept aside as Rachel nearly throttled her in a bear hug while Sam and Louise eyed each other shyly.

They drove home, making superficial comments about how good it was to see each other, how bad the traffic was and that Timothy had gone to Rachel's parents for the weekend for the first time. As she passed their church, Joanna pointed it out and commented on how happy they were there, and that she was now a member of the PCC. Rachel raised her eyebrows but said nothing. Joanna noticed, but decided this wasn't the time to ask.

After a late dinner, Louise and Sam went happily together to Louise's bedroom to play, Matthew demanded help with his maths homework from Stephen, and Andrew went to play computer games. Joanna and Rachel settled down with steaming mugs of coffee and started to talk. They reminisced about college, reminding each other of some of the escapades they'd been involved in. They talked about the boyfriends they'd had before Joanna met Stephen and Rachel got to know Mike. Gradually they began to open up and share what their lives were really like now.

Rachel and Mike had both done very well in their jobs, and a year or so before had moved to a village a few miles from the town where they worked. Sam had quickly settled into the village school, and was thriving in the small class she was in there. She'd found a superb child-minder for Timothy, and Sam went to the same woman before and after school.

The only down side of the move was the church. They felt they ought to worship where they lived, and so had happily turned up at the local parish church on their first Sunday. The congregation had been mostly elderly people, but there was one other family, also with two young children, who'd been delighted to welcome others their own age. She'd found it pretty hard work keeping Sam and Timothy quiet at first, but they'd soon worked out a strategy to cope.

Eventually Rachel asked the question Joanna had been waiting for – how come she was on the PCC?

'Why not?' Joanna responded, not quite knowing Rachel's reason for the question. Rachel poured out the story of their recent church experience.

All had gone well at church until Rachel wanted to start a Sunday School, initially for the four children, but she had hoped that others in the village might come. She had talked to Mike, discussed her ideas with the other family and found out about possible materials before going to see the vicar. To her amazement he poured cold water on the whole idea. It would have to be approved by the PCC, who would also decide who would teach. Nor was there any money for materials or the alterations he was sure would be needed to meet safety standards. After about ten minutes she found herself outside again.

She had been furious. How dare anyone treat her like that! She had charged round to see Agnes, an elderly lady in the church who had befriended them. She poured out her story, expecting Agnes to agree that she had been unjustly treated. To her amazement, Agnes sided with the vicar, and remarked that while she might be free to come up with ideas and implement them at work, it was a different matter at church. The vicar made decisions, and there hadn't been a Sunday School for 20 years because the vicar wanted all leadership roles to be taken by men. None of the men had been willing to take responsibility for leading the Sunday School, because they thought that it was women's work.

Rachel had hardly been able to believe her ears – were there really people who still held attitudes like that in this day and age? They'd never get away with it in a business context. Joanna could see she was still smarting, but also confused by the refusal of what had been a perfectly genuine offer. She had heard that there were vicars like Rachel and Mike's, but she hadn't come face to face with the problem before.

* * * * *

We saw in the last chapter that problems for women in the church can arise from various sources:

- Theological convictions that women should not take leadership roles

- The structures of the church which were de-
  vised by men and have been almost exclusively
  run by them for centuries
- A misplaced sense of power on the behalf of
  some church leaders
- An unwillingness by some older people to
  change traditional attitudes.

How often do women actually face problems such as
Rachel's these days? There were a number of women
in the research groups who said that the gifts they
had which they felt could be used in the church were
either not used at all, or only in a minimal way. The
reasons they gave for this were much more often the
ones we've already looked at: lack of confidence, a
non-believing husband or too much else going on in
their life to make it realistic.

However, there were some who said the reason
lay with the church and not with them. You may remember that many in the research groups had
dropped out of church for at least a year at some
point in their adult lives. One of the women had
done so when she found herself in a similar position
to Rachel. It was some time before she returned, and
then she deliberately chose a Methodist church, as
this denomination had given more freedom to lay
people, including women, right from its earliest
days. There were others who ran into opposition to
the use of their gifts, especially in churches where the
leadership was exclusively male and there seemed to
be the desire to keep it that way.

Women's reactions to not being able to use their gifts

Frustration

Women have been frustrated for many years by what seems to be 'double-think' in some churches. It's very obvious in relation to women missionaries. Many women serve God faithfully as missionaries in all sorts of capacities. Some of them fulfil traditional women's roles in hospitals and schools, while others plant new churches, preach and teach, and may be in responsible positions in an emerging church. It is quite common for the more experienced missionaries to be older single women, the married couples having returned home to find suitable secondary schooling for their children. It is especially frustrating for such women to come home, either for a break between periods overseas, or at the end of their missionary service, to find that although their home church had happily prayed for them and supported them in their work overseas, when they want to do the same kind of things at home there is an invisible wall that stops them.

It is equally frustrating for able, mature women like Rachel with positions of senior leadership at work to find that their abilities and gifts are not acceptable in the church. They are seen as out of place, or perhaps a threat to the way a church has 'always' functioned. We've already discovered that such women may eventually find themselves unable to remain in church any longer.

While there are undoubtedly many churches where women are free to exercise whatever gifts they have, there are others where the doors of opportunity are closed. The problem not only arises with upfront leadership, but with any role which involves a woman having some sort of responsibility, especially over men. One of the younger women in our survey had run into this issue when she moved to a new church when she started her first job. She openly said that if she hadn't moved church within a year or two, she probably wouldn't be going any more. Another found that whenever she did do anything, even as simple as taking a reading, she received sarcastic comments from one or two men in particular. She was discouraged, and felt she was unlikely to agree next time she was asked.

Feeling irrelevant

As one woman put it,

> Anyone can make tea, you don't need a 'gift' to do it, nor do you need to be a woman. Many women want to use their gifts, not just do the jobs they are capable of.

If a woman's gifts are not recognized and she is not allowed to use them in a fulfilling way to serve God and the church, she may not be willing to do anything. Someone who is a gifted bible teacher but is never allowed to preach or even to lead a home bible study group may eventually decide either to move to a church where her gifts are welcome, or to opt out of taking any active part in church life at all.

Women seem to react with the feeling that if their gifts are not welcome, then they as people are not welcome. This appears to be especially true of women who do not exercise their gifts in any other context, whether at work, in an environment such as the Women's Institute or in charitable work of some kind. In effect, such women are silenced, and squeezed out of any significant role in the life and work of the church.

Voicelessness

There is a deeper kind of silencing which is sometimes referred to by its effect – 'voicelessness'. This occurs where people do not have involvement in the decision-making process and have to accept decisions made by others on their behalf. This results in them feeling that as far as the people who make decisions are concerned, it is almost as though they didn't exist. An often-quoted example is that of an anthropologist who had been studying the way of life of a group of people. He wrote, 'The next day, all the villagers sailed away aboard some thirty canoes, leaving us behind, alone with the women and children in the abandoned houses.' For this writer, only the men were 'villagers' – they had 'all' gone and the houses were described as 'abandoned', and yet the women and children were still there![1]

For some women in the church this is particularly true. Sister Lavinia Byrne, a well-known broadcaster who regularly speaks on radio programmes such as *Thought for the Day* on BBC Radio 4's *Today*, made a decision at the beginning of January 2000 that she must leave her religious order. Her reason for doing so was that she had been continuously under pressure since writing a book about the issue of women priests and the Roman Catholic Church. She described her experience as 'being silenced', and felt she could no longer keep quiet about a subject she believed should be a matter of open debate.[2]

It is this sense of not being listened to and of a particular perspective being ignored which has led in the last forty or fifty years to the development of particular theological movements. Liberation Theology, developed in the 1960s, principally in Latin American Roman Catholic circles, attempts to unite theology and problems of poverty and social injustice. Black Theology, originating among black people in America and Africa, is committed to the improvement of the status of black people in the face of racism. Feminist Theology, a movement begun by women and for women, works to reintroduce a female perspective. Because of what are seen as patriarchal attitudes in the church, many women feel a sense of voicelessness, especially – but not only – those who have been influenced by feminism. The philosopher Mary Midgley offers an explanation of why a woman's viewpoint could be seen to not matter: 'From the ancient hierarchical point of view ... it could not matter because women themselves did not really matter. They were in effect an inferior kind of man, with no distinctive character of their own.'[3]

In contrast, there are apparently some evangelical churches in Latin America where the women have become so powerful that they have in effect silenced the men. This situation arose out of a different kind of voicelessness, which had been experienced by members of protestant churches in some parts of South America where Roman Catholicism is particularly dominant. Where protestants were not allowed to preach or evangelize publicly, they sometimes found a warm welcome among women in their homes, who therefore became the majority in new churches that were established.[4]

Marginalization

In some churches there are unspoken assumptions which make women feel marginalized. There may be no stated policy which says that deacons or PCC members or their equivalent have to be men. It's simply that any women who are suggested don't get elected. There is a similar problem with appointing young people to leadership positions in church, which shows that the issue isn't always so much a gender-based one as an unwillingness to change the *status quo*.

However, sometimes such assumptions of marginalization are made by women themselves. One person I interviewed who speaks at conferences which aim to encourage and support women said:

> Women who come to conferences say, 'If only I could do this in my church . . . ' They may be allowed to do it, but perceive that some men disapprove deep down, even though they don't say so. Women feel the negative vibes and say they aren't allowed to do certain things, which they actually may be able to.

Her desire was to encourage women to have the courage to test the barriers and see if they could be broken down.

Both men and women may be making assumptions, and it can become a 'chicken-and-egg' situation, with women thinking the men won't let them, while the men think the women don't want to.

The difficulty is that these kinds of attitudes are damaging the church. They lead to people's gifts being suppressed and, at worst, to women leaving the church. Rob Warner put it like this:

> Women are still all too often marginalised. Attitudes that would be unlawful in the workplace are still accepted and even found amusing in many churches. Many women feel marginalised and patronised. Their views are not taken seriously and their gifts are under-utilised. Younger women have many searching questions, for example about juggling the demands of career and child-care, that are simply not addressed by the kind of church that is locked into 1950s stereotypes, presenting a standardised role for every woman.[5]

Perceptions

A fascinating picture emerged in the survey from which the original issues for this research project were extracted. One question asked both men and women what leadership roles men and women took in their church. The intention was that men would fill in what the men did, while women filled in what the women did. However, as the instructions were ambiguous, both men and women answered both questions. The result was that we could see what women said they did and what men thought women did, as well as what men said they did and what women thought they did. As these surveys were filled in by most if not all the people in a congregation, it is fairly safe to assume that people were accurate in what they replied about their own involvement in church activities. But what was very interesting was what women replied to the question asking what men did in their church, and vice versa.

The women had a pretty good idea of what the men were doing in their church – their answers were very similar to the men's, although they were likely to perceive men as doing slightly fewer practical tasks such as coffee mornings, lunches and working with the elderly.

Not so the men's answers about what they thought the women in their church did! Perhaps not surprisingly, women were more involved than men in coffee mornings, church lunches, working with young families or the elderly, counselling and women's meetings. The men got the amount of work women did in these areas about right, although they didn't think women did as much counselling and visiting as the women said they did.

The fascinating finding was when we looked at the activities in which fewer women were involved: leading services, preaching and in leadership roles such as the PCC or diaconate. In these areas of church life men said women did *more*, sometimes much more, than the women said they did! There could be at least two possible reasons for this.

Perhaps men think they've given women the opportunities to take up these roles and so assume they are
doing them. More likely in many churches is that
women are less likely to be involved in these roles
and so men notice much more when a woman, say,
preaches than when a man does. When asked how
much involvement women have in these activities,
their instinctive reaction is that it must be 'quite a lot'
because they are more aware when it does happen.

FACT BOX

Another survey bears out that fewer women than men
serve on their church's PCC, diaconate or eldership, but
that the more people there are in such groups, the more
likely it is that at least one member will be a woman,
with larger PCCs being made up of roughly half men
and half women.[6]

The answers to this question showed, unfortunately,
that gender stereotyping is still alive and well in
many churchgoers' attitudes. It's much stronger
among male churchgoers than female, but we
women suffer from it a little also. It was a fairly extreme example of this that Rachel faced from Agnes
when she went to her for support after the vicar refused to let her start a Sunday School. Agnes just did
not think it appropriate for Rachel to take on such a
role, and in this she probably saw herself as uphold-
ing traditional roles and values. Older women are
more likely than any other group to feel a job is most
suitable for the gender that have traditionally undertaken it – male car mechanics and female secretaries

for example,[7] and older women in the church are just as likely to hold similar views.

However, Agnes's response raises another issue, because she didn't only express her own views, she also backed up the vicar – if he thought women shouldn't take on leadership roles, then there was no point discussing it. Even with the ordination of women in the Church of England most people's experience of church is still one of exclusively or predominantly male leadership. Many men in church leadership have never had a woman working as a leader either over them or with them, and therefore may not have had their prejudices challenged.

Women in the Christian community

When Christian Research was planning this research project we surveyed our own members, asking a range of questions about women.[8] 478 members replied, and it is worth spending a few minutes looking at some of their answers.

How many churches actually had a woman minister? It was quite clear that the likelihood increased when the church had more than one minister.

This table shows that smaller churches were much less likely to have a woman minister, and that a woman was much less likely to work on her own as the only minister in a church. Where there was only one minister in a church (46% of all churches), 92% were male, which corresponded with the national average of 8% of ministers being women in 1995.[9] By 2000 10.4% of the 34,000 ministers in the UK were

Table 1: *Number of ministers per church, and proportion who are women*

Number of ministers	Proportion of churches %	Proportion with at least one woman %
None	13	n/a
One	46	8
Two	23	29
Three	10	46
Four	4	55
Five or more	4	89

women, and it is expected to reach to almost 12% by 2005.[10]

This is in direct contrast to charities. The smaller the charity, the more likely it is that the chief executive will be a woman, especially in charities with an annual income of less that £1 million a year and fewer than 20 staff. The issue would appear to be responsibility. A woman is less likely to have sole responsibility for a church, but rather to be part of a team in a larger church. She is also less likely to have senior responsibility in a large charity, but again to be part of a senior management team.[11]

Christian Research members were also asked how they felt about working with women. The questions were answered by some people in relation to the church and by others in relation to their workplace, whether secular or a Christian organization. The answers were fairly similar, so they have all been put together here, and only the questions with a reasonable number of responses have been included.

Two-thirds of these people enjoyed working with a woman, which interestingly is more than the percentage who enjoy having a woman working for them. However, only a quarter enjoyed working for a woman. What is more worrying is the 10% who approve in principle to working for a woman, but dislike it personally, and the 9% who would prefer not to work for a woman if they could avoid it. Although these last two are relatively small percentages, nevertheless they do represent nearly 1 in 5 men, and demonstrate deep-seated attitudes which are

Table 2: *Attitudes of respondents when working with women*

	Working for a woman %	Working with a woman %	Women working for you %	Overall %
Enjoy it	28	62	50	47
Not bothered one way or the other	44	42	44	43
Prefer it	1	12	7	7
Approve in principle but dislike personally	10	1	1	4
Prefer not to if could avoid it	9	1	1	4

likely to lead to the sort of frustrations and assumptions which we have just been considering.

These issues were explored further in a series of statements to which people had five choices of response varying from 'strongly agree' to 'strongly disagree'. Two statements received warm approval, putting together those who 'strongly agree' and 'agree':

- I welcome women in leadership and value their contribution (87% agreed).
- The church has been influenced by society to undervalue the gifts of women (61% agreed).

The next two statements received an even spread of answers, with roughly the same number agreeing as disagreeing or opting to sit on the fence:

- Because the church's agenda is set entirely by men, it does not meet the needs of women (29% agreed, 42% disagreed).
- I don't disapprove of women ministers, but personally I'd rather be led by a man (26% agreed, 53% disagreed).

The people in this survey strongly disagreed with the last two statements, adding together those who 'disagree' and 'strongly disagree'. In other words, they *didn't* agree either that women should be subordinate, or that they should never be church leaders:

- Women can be church leaders, just so long as they are subordinate to men (68%).

- The Bible makes it clear that women should never be church leaders (76%).

Again, the concern is not so much with the majority who agree with the first pair of statements, but with the small minority who disagree with welcoming women in leadership and valuing their contribution, as well as those who either agree or sit on the fence about preferring to be led by a man. Perhaps these are the same people who create the 'glass ceilings' in churches.

One of the 'gurus' of human resource development, Brian Molitor, has written:

> More and more women are rising to leadership positions throughout the world and are performing extremely well. It has been fun to watch the response from their male counterparts. Some men have patronised and some have fraternised with their new colleagues. Others have tried to ignore them, hoping they would leave. Others have tried to sabotage the careers of women in order to 'purify' the ranks of their company. Fortunately, most have accepted the infusion of women into the workplace for what it actually is: the addition of an extremely valuable resource into a business world that needs all the help it can get.[12]

It is clear that a similar range of reactions occurs in the church, with the added complication of theological issues. Perhaps some of the same solutions will help us along the way towards working together and valuing one another's gifts more. Brian Molitor makes the following suggestions:

For women:
- Be the person you were created to be
- Retain your femininity and the caring that normally sets women apart from men
- Listen – once – to your critics to determine their motivation and see if they have anything valuable to say
- Learn to forgive those that are fearful, critical, and spiteful of you
- Protect your health
- Keep your priorities in order
- Take time for yourself.

For men:
- Relax and reflect on the impact that other people who were different had when they first entered your work environment
- Realize that you will need a period of adjustment
- Control your imaginations and feelings about women in the workplace
- Remain professional
- Evaluate the performance of women using the same standards as you use for other men
- Accept the subtle differences between men and women.

But are these Biblical answers to the difficulties that can arise when men and women start working together? Reflect on them for a moment, and you may see that they are remarkably biblical. God created us who we are. He wants us to accept and when necessary forgive others on the same basis as he does – we pray 'forgive us our debts as we also have forgiven our debtors' (Mt. 6:12). He asks us to love our neighbour as ourself.

It seems unlikely that we will ever rid the church completely of all prejudice because we are all human. But showing acceptance and grace toward one another can gradually break down many of those prejudices more effectively than a confrontational approach. And that is not the same as being a doormat, sitting back and allowing the prejudices to continue. There is evidence that church people, especially those who work alongside women in their workplace, are recognizing that roles depend not on gender or age but on gifting. If you are in a church where you do not have freedom to use your gifts, may God give you grace to find a way through the 'glass ceiling'.

FOR FURTHER THOUGHT

1 Have you ever been in a situation similar to Rachel, or do you know someone who has? What effect has the situation had on your attitudes towards church?
2 Are you regularly made to feel frustrated, irrelevant, voiceless or marginalized in your church? Do you know if other women feel the same? Can you get together to pray about the situation and support one another in it?
3 How do you respond to Brian Molitor's suggestions for women on page 142? Are there any of these which you need to take action on especially?

Notes

1 Originally written by Levi-Strauss and quoted in Martin Soskice, Janet 'The Silence of the Ma'ams', *Leading Light*, Vol. 1, 1993, pp. 10–11.

2 Reported in most national daily newspapers, 11 Jan. 2000.

3 Janet Martin Soskice, *Leading Light*, Vol. 1, 1993, pp. 10–11.

4 Martin, David, *Tongues of Fire: The Explosion of Protestantism in Latin America* (Oxford: Basil Blackwell, 1990), pp. 181–4.

5 Warner, Rob, 'Create a Church From Scratch', *Renewal*, March 1999, p. 45.

6 Christian Research, *Women in the Christian Community*, survey of Christian Research members, 1996, p.7.

7 Witherspoon, Sharon, 'Sex Roles and Gender Issues', *British Social Attitudes*, report by Social and Community Planning Research (Aldershot: Gower Publishing Company Ltd., 1985), pp. 65–77.

8 Christian Research, *Women in the Christian Community*.

9 Brierley, Peter and Wraight, Heather (eds.), *UK Christian Handbook, 1996/1997* (London: Christian Research, 1995), table 9b, p. 240.

10 Brierley, Peter, *Religious Trends 2002/2003* (London: Christian Research, 2001), page 2.21

11 Dalton, Dorothy, *Gender and Chief Executives in the Voluntary Sector* (London: ACENVO, 1997).

12 Moliter, Brian, 'Women Are Here To Stay', *Ethos*, Dec. 1999/Jan. 2000, p. 12.

8

Getting There From Here

Saturday was a beautiful day, so Joanna and Stephen made plans for a picnic. Matthew had a lot of homework and now he was 14 wanted to be allowed more freedom and independence. After some discussion it was agreed that he could stay at home on his own. Soon after breakfast Stephen and Andrew set off for the school football match. They would meet up at their favourite picnic spot later in the morning. Rachel helped Joanna pack up a box of goodies, while Sam and Louise played in the garden. Old Bessie's face wrinkled with delight when she saw her doggie dinner being prepared.

It didn't take long to get everything ready. As they drove through the town Rachel remarked on the number of churches they passed. She loved living in a village, but after her conversation with Joanna last night she wondered whether choosing to go to the parish church with its traditional attitudes had actually been best for her family. What would it mean spiritually for her and Mike as the years passed? Would their faith grow in that kind of soil? At seven, Sam was already complaining about church being boring, and was it really worth the hassle of keeping Timothy occupied and quiet?

She was taken aback by these thoughts. It was funny how she thought through every possible angle of a decision at work, and yet when it came to church she realized she hadn't considered lots of things. She had been surprised last night by how much more thoughtful and mature Joanna had seemed than last time they met. Obviously the move had made Joanna face up to issues that she and Mike had somehow ignored when they had moved. It had created a restlessness in her – not necessarily to change to another church, but certainly to see some spiritual growth in their lives.

It wasn't long before they reached a delightful spot on the bank of a bubbling stream. They unpacked the picnic things and spread out a blanket on the soft grass. The girls quickly pulled off their sandals, rolled up their trousers and set about trying to dam the stream. Rachel started to voice her thoughts to Joanna. 'You seem much happier, and somehow more settled than when we last met. What's brought about the change?'

Joanna was surprised at first. Then as she cast her mind back over the recent months she realized it was true. Slowly at first she explored what had been happening in her life. Rachel listened, fascinated, as Joanna talked about the struggles to find the right church, and the realization that perhaps at this stage of life they might need something different spiritually as the children grew up. They chatted about the difficulties of really feeling accepted among strangers, and the friendships they were each beginning to form. Matthew still being willing to come to church had been a major answer to prayer for Joanna, which had encouraged her to pray more about other circumstances in her life. Taking her turn leading the home group had made her do some in-depth preparation that had done her good too – she'd rather let her mind go fallow since the children were babies. And being elected to the PCC had helped her apply her faith to a wider range of issues.

The more she rambled on, musing out loud to Rachel, the more Joanna realized that, yes, she did somehow feel more alive spiritually than she had done a year ago. She wasn't quite sure how to describe it, and used phrases like her faith had grown, her relationship with God had deepened and she had moved on in her spiritual journey.

* * * * *

Growing in faith

If you were asked whether your faith had grown in the last year, how would you reply? Would you immediately respond with a 'yes' or 'no'? Perhaps the question would set you thinking, rather like Rachel. Or maybe you would instinctively answer 'yes' but not quite know why, which was Joanna's initial response. In the survey of churches from which the issues for this research were drawn, more women than men in every church said their faith had grown 'much' or 'some' in the last year. In the research groups a similar pattern emerged, with more than half the women saying their faith had grown in the last year.

Saying faith has grown doesn't mean very much without being able to explain in what ways. There were several factors, and as with other aspects of this research, they turned out to be a mixture of spiritual and practical aspects.

Relationship with God

Several women described a feeling of knowing God better. Perhaps it was a deeper understanding of who He is, or a growing recognition of his love for them and acceptance of them. For others it was a greater awareness of his presence; a sense that he was with them all the time and not only when they were worshipping him in church. One woman said

I can talk to God more, about anything.' Another woman commented, 'I know him better and understand better his ways in my life,' and another, 'I have a greater peace that God is in control.

God is a person, and as in any other deepening relationship the more we get to know him, the closer we feel to him. There is a desire to include him in all that we do. For some, there is an awareness that he's there alongside us on the good and the bad days. Others have the freedom to chat to him about everything that's going on as though he were actually there – which as Christians we believe he is!

Increased responsibilities

For some women their faith had grown because they had been stretched. They had taken on a new responsibility in church, or a Christian service, like Joanna leading the home group on some occasions and being elected to the PCC. Sometimes they had offered to take on a new task, as Joanna and Stephen did when they talked to the vicar. For others the new job was taken on in response to a request, perhaps one to which they initially wanted to say no, but then did agree to.

It doesn't seem to matter what the task is, rather our motive for doing it. The story is told of a man who visited a stonemason's yard when a great cathedral was being built. He asked various masons what they were doing as they worked on their piece of stone. One replied, 'Making this stone smooth,' another, 'Carving the top of a pillar.' But one answered, 'Building a cathedral for God.' Whether the new task is tidying up the churchyard or preaching for the first time, growth in faith happens when that job is seen as 'for God' rather than any other reason.

Often a new task makes us more dependent on God. For example, starting to teach Sunday School for the first time can be daunting, but overcoming the apprehension and finding God is there to help can be an experience which helps our faith to grow. Similarly, carrying on with a task which is difficult when we'd like to give up but know God doesn't want us to, also makes us more dependent on him and can help our faith grow.

Answered prayer

One of Joanna's encouragements had been an answered prayer for Matthew. He was still willing to come to church and had found friends there. Having our prayers answered is a great encouragement to faith. We all know that not all our prayers are answered in the way we expect! But when they are, it is a real boost to pray about other things. This means that we need to pray in such a way so as to recognize when our prayers are answered. Jill Briscoe describes what she calls 'Christopher Robin prayers', from the poem by A.A. Milne in which the second verse starts, 'God bless Mummy. I know that's right. Wasn't it fun in the bath tonight?' In other words, a short, routine prayer has no obvious answer to it, as Jill found:

> When I first became a committed believer at the age of eighteen, I began to pray Christopher Robin prayers. 'God bless Africa', I intoned fervently at one memorable prayer meeting. A mature Christian came up to me afterward and inquired, 'Which part of that great continent is your concern?' . . . I realised 'God bless Africa' was not going to be sufficient![1]

Specific answers to prayer had helped people in the research grow in their faith. Those answers might have been for themselves or for their family or friends, but they were very practical and personal prayers. Being able to thank God for the answer was a point of spiritual growth.

Times of crisis

The nature of a crisis can vary enormously. It could be problems with a child, health difficulties, being made redundant, a personality clash at work or church, the death of a parent or any one of the multitudes of crises which affect us all at some point in our lives.

Churches are families, and like any other family they have their good times and bad times. The church is not immune from problems and difficulties. Unfortunately things can go wrong, sometimes very badly wrong. We can face crises there too, either corporately or individually.

Will such unwelcome events rule your life and drive a wedge between you and God? Or will they send you running to him for help and support? Coping with a crisis is very demanding, but it can also be a point of spiritual growth.

Confidence to share my faith

Many of us find it hard to talk about our faith, and yet underneath would love our friends and neighbours to know God in the way we do. Taking an opportunity to do this, perhaps in a very simple way, was one of the factors in helping faith to grow. It might be inviting someone to come to church with you, or being more open about what you believe in day-to-day conversations. Some churches run courses which are appropriate for non-churchgoers, and it is a great encouragement when a friend accepts an invitation to one.[2]

Friendship

Faith also grew for some because of one particular friend, or the friendship and support of a group

such as a home group. Having a Christian friend
with whom to talk about matters of faith was a significant help for a number of women. Here was
someone with whom they could discuss their long-
ings and hopes, doubts and questions, and someone
to pray with and be encouraged by; someone to say,
'How are you getting on with that problem you told
me about last week?', a friend to phone and say,
'Help, please pray. We've got a crisis.' This friendship is two-way. It is just as encouraging to faith if
you are on the other end of the phone and know
that someone has trusted you to be there for them in
a time of need. Seeing how they cope can bolster
your faith that in a similar crisis God will be there
for you too. It was this kind of challenge which
awakened Rachel to the fact that her own faith
might not be growing, while Joanna's was.

Teaching

Relevant teaching on the Christian faith was a clear
reason why some women's faith had grown. Sometimes the source was a particularly appropriate sermon or series of sermons. For others there had been
the opportunity to go to one of the many Christian
conferences or holidays available these days. Reading a book was the stimulus for some, while for others it was reading the Bible. The common factor was
that a deeper knowledge of God or some specific aspect of the Christian life had helped their faith to
grow.

Attitude

Some women couldn't point to specific answers to prayer, new responsibilities, or describe in what way their relationship with God had deepened. Nevertheless they still knew instinctively that their faith had grown. It might be a feeling of 'enjoying' their faith more – feeling more 'alive' during worship, or sensing God's presence more often. Faith doesn't only grow in difficult times!

For the women in this study, growth in faith and relationships were bound together. If relationships within their church were going well, then it was likely that their relationship with God would also go well, and that their faith would grow. Equally, if her relationship with God was strong, a woman's relationships with others were affected positively. However, the same was true the other way round. If relationships were going wrong then faith was affected, and if a woman's relationship with God was not good then other relationships might be less positive also.

When faith doesn't grow

There were, inevitably, some women who felt their faith hadn't grown. Some of them were clearly envious of those in the group who were describing their experiences of growth. It was hard for some to open up publicly and say why, and I am very grateful to those who had the courage to do so and so help us all.

Listening to the factors which helped faith to grow clarified for some why their faith hadn't grown. Perhaps a particularly important prayer hadn't been answered – a friend had died of cancer, or a child had got into bad company. For others a crisis had damaged their faith and made them feel they couldn't trust God because he didn't appear to have helped them at all. Another wished she had been asked to take on a new responsibility. She felt ignored and undervalued in her church, and this sense of being a non-person had extended to feeling that God viewed her in the same way. Several expressed the fact that there was a lack of teaching in their church, so there was no challenge to grow spiritually. It was easy to lose the motivation to keep working at faith when that faith didn't seem to be encouraged by going to church.

An older lady commented that she wasn't sure she expected her faith to grow. Her relationship with God was good, she enjoyed going to church, she had plenty of friends in her various church activities, and there were no major crises in life. She was quite happy to be where she was spiritually.

What would it take for those whose faith wasn't growing for it to start to grow again? For some people the answer to this was practical. Perhaps a reordering of priorities to allow more time to read the Bible or Christian books and to pray. For another it was seeing the children more settled in Sunday School so she could concentrate on the service and meet with God rather than be constantly distracted by her youngsters.

One woman longed for a new challenge – even recognizing this may have helped her to go away and look for one. Perhaps that challenge would come through taking on a new task in the church, but it could also be through a friend. Friendships can help us just as much, possibly more, when we are low spiritually as when things are going well. If you have a friend who is struggling spiritually at the moment, what could you do to encourage or even challenge her? Simply being there in a non-judgmental way to listen, support and encourage can be enough. As one woman said, 'We don't listen to each other enough,' especially in the hard times.

Seeing God answer prayer is another way to kick-start fresh spiritual growth. Interestingly, it doesn't necessarily have to be your own prayers which are answered! It might be corporate prayer at church, a friend's prayer, or those of your children.

For others the need went much deeper. They had been hurt spiritually, and a great deal of healing, support and perhaps counsel would be needed if their faith was to turn around and become positive again. Perhaps these are the people who, if I went back to talk to them again a year on, I would find are no longer going to church. The rewards of faith and the encouragement to press on are missing, and without these they are asking the question whether it is possible to continue. These are the people whom we most need to be aware of in our churches, and yet they feel themselves the least loved and cared for. How can we identify such people, and reach out to them in love and support?

A secure faith

A growing faith is likely to lead to other positive benefits in our spiritual lives. It will make us more eager to attend church, like a hungry person wanting to have a meal.

> **FACT BOX**
>
> People who attend church at least once a month are much more likely to have a growing faith than those who attend less often.[3]

Surveys of people in local congregations reveal three factors linked statistically with going to church at least once a month.[4] One is a faith which is growing, which was explored in more depth in the women's research. The second is experiencing the presence of God in worship. The third is a willingness to share faith. Coming to church more often helps us to experience God's presence in worship. This encourages our faith to grow, which leads to a willingness to share it because we feel positive about our relationship with God. In turn, sharing our faith helps it to grow, resulting in more willingness to share it, eagerness to come to church and openness to experience God's presence!

It would be interesting to know which is the prime motivating one factor, although it is likely to be different factors for different people. These three factors suggest that people who come to church regularly have a more secure faith, which they are confident enough to share.

Experiencing the presence of God

To say you experience the presence of God can seem weird to people who have never done so. Is it some sort of warm glow in the pit of the stomach? Or like a ghost flitting past? No. It's more like the sixth sense that a mother has about her newborn child: an antenna that alerts her to the baby.

People described this sense in phrases like these:

- 'A feeling of peace and excitement all at the same time
- 'A feeling of peace and power, often at communion when I take the bread and wine
- 'A sense of encouragement, even if nothing particularly encouraging has been said
- 'An awareness that God is more important than the people around me
- 'An awareness of the Holy Spirit moving in me, touching deep inside me
- 'An intuitive "knowing" that he has heard my prayer
- 'Like God putting his arm round me and telling me he loves me
- 'A sense that there is someone there, whom I want to reach out to
- 'A sudden alertness to God in creation
- 'Knowing that he is in control of my life and his purpose is being fulfilled
- 'When I'm asking him for guidance and suddenly I know what to do

- 'For younger women: empowerment; for older women a feeling of belonging, of being fathered
- 'A conviction that he's OK and I'm OK.'

These statements are very strongly biased towards feelings and emotions. Some literature on spirituality suggests that women are more likely to feel the presence of God than men. I asked the women I interviewed if they thought it was true. They all agreed, though in different ways. Women do appear to be more sensitive to emotions and relationships, and therefore expect to experience their faith in those dimensions, perhaps more than men do. It is partly to do with temperament, and we must recognize that some women are less emotional and some men more so. But in general women tend to be more subjective and intuitive. They don't necessarily need a logical explanation for something before they can accept it. It is difficult to describe the presence of God, but that doesn't stop us experiencing it.

This is one of the areas in the research where it is really frustrating not to know what men think. Do they experience the presence of God in the same ways? Asking around among friends suggests not, perhaps partly because they don't expect to do so in the same way a woman might. Their faith seems to be based more on facts, on learning about God rather than feeling his presence, and so feeling this is not something they necessarily expect as part of their faith:

Abstract reason has, for the long history of Western thought, been ascribed to men, while women have been thought to be emotional, that is, irrational. We need to recognise that to be human is to be capable both of reason and of emotional engagement.[5]

Perhaps we women can help more men to experience the presence of God in their lives, and so encourage them in their faith!

Faith as a journey

It was quite clear that growing in faith meant different things to different people, especially at the various stages of life. I often challenge the pre-teens I know to allow their faith to grow up as they grow up. A 12-year-old's faith isn't robust enough to withstand the pressures of being 16 or 17. My faith at 40 was not at all like my faith at 20. God meets us where we are, at whatever stage of life we are living through. Reading some of David's psalms reminds us of that. In some psalms he is wildly elated by his relationship with God, in others he is in the depths of despair. But his trust in God shines through in each situation.

In recent years it has become much more common to describe this growth in faith as a journey. It's not a new idea! Both biblical teaching and Christian tradition remind us again and again that faith is a constant learning and growing process. Describing faith as a journey is easy to understand, and one most churchgoers seem to feel comfortable with. Life changes and for our faith to be relevant it needs to change and develop too.

Several people have attempted to describe the sort of stages we may go through as our faith grows. If you haven't come across these examples before, you may find them helpful to enable you to recognize where you are now and how you might grow. They aren't like a mathematical formula: $a + b = c$, so that stage one plus stage two equals stage three, or even like Shakespeare's seven ages of man which all of us go through if we live long enough. They're more descriptions of the way people experience faith. They're useful if they encourage us when we see how far we've come, or if looking at aspects of faith we haven't yet experienced challenges us to move on spiritually. The three examples given below demonstrate quite different approaches to which different people relate according to their personality and approach to faith.

Engel's scale

Able to teach others		+5
Mature Christian		+4
New Christian		+2
Decision to follow Christ	■	+1
Understands way of salvation		−2
Understands some basics of the Gospel		−5
Initial exposure to the Gospel		−8
Knows nothing about the Gospel		−10

This scale moves upwards from the bottom. It takes as its basis Jesus' command to 'make disciples' (Mt. 28:19) and considers the process needed to take someone from no knowledge of the Christian faith right through the discipleship stages until they are able to begin the cycle again by in turn making disciples. It is often used by evangelicals and considers what communication will need to take place.[6]

This scale only deals with the knowledge that people gain about the Christian faith. Another scale running horizontally has been added to this vertical scale which adds an emotional dimension, something like this:

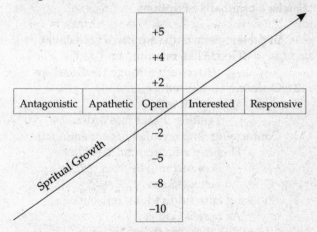

Put the two together and the process of growth towards Christian maturity requires a change in both directions. So, for example, someone may know quite a lot about the Christian faith but be very antagonistic towards it. Such a person is not, at this point in their life anyway, growing towards a mature Christian faith. On the other hand, someone who knows very little but longs to know more, and in that sense is responsive, may progress very quickly as a Christian.

Fowler's stages of faith

James Fowler approached the question of how our faith grows in a quite different way, by using the ideas of developmental psychologists. His aim was to demonstrate that life experiences and growth in faith go hand in hand.[7] The words in brackets are Fowler's original descriptions.

1   Impressionistic faith (intuitive/projective)
            'God is like my mum and dad' –
                 discovery through relationships
2   Ordering faith (mythical/literal)
            'What's fair is fair' –
                 getting things into order
3   Conforming faith (synthetic/conventional)
            'I believe what the church believes' –
                 conforming to other people's
                 expectations
4   Choosing faith (individual/reflective)
            'As I see it God is . . .' –
                 thinking things through
5   Balanced faith (conjunctive)
            'Distinguishing the map from the
                 territory' – seeing a broader
                 picture, especially in relation to
                 emotions

6   Selfless faith (universalizing)
        'I have a dream' – the big vision.

Intimacy with God

Glen Martin and Dian Ginter found themselves frequently being asked how one can grow closer to God, so they wrote a book to share what they had learned in their own relationships with him. They identified six levels of intimacy with God, pointing out that progressing through them is not by way of magic formulae, but rather by working at certain areas of faith in order to grow spiritually. For example, at times of dryness or testing we may move back a level or two but our aim should be to grow closer to God.[8]

If these three ways of looking at growing in faith don't appeal to you, don't worry. Perhaps they are too abstract, too logical, or even too masculine! The important thing is not what method you use to describe your spiritual journey, but that you are on one. Can you look back and say your faith has grown in the last year? If not, may I encourage you to examine why, and take steps to move on. Decide now to take time to do this. It will not only help you, but also your family and friends, and others in your church.

God as ⟋ Aspects of Christian Life	Level 1 Holy Sovereign	Level 2 Forgiving Saviour
Qualities of God important at this stage	Creator, majestic, holy, King, eternal	Good, loving, merciful, forgiving
Obedience based on . . .	Fear	Thankfulness, gratitude
Closeness to God	Arm's length	Kneeling in surrender
Heart's response	Curiosity, worship, awe	Thankful, loving, desire to obey
Focus of prayer	Self-centred	Duty, love
Effect of actions with others	Limited	Mainly self-centred
Outlook on life	Self-centred, insecure	Anticipation

Level 3 Loving Father	Level 4 Faithful Companion	Level 5 Good Friend	Level 6 Intimate Friend
Protector, teacher, kind, accepting	Compassion- ate, wonderful, faithful	Wisdom, purity, unchanging, comforter	Absolute sovereign, gentle, trustworthy
Necessity	Love	Deep love, desire to do God's will	Pleasing God always
Can 'touch' him	Hand in hand	Arm in arm	Inseparable
Growing trust, feeling of belonging	Deepening love and trust	Desire to obey completely	Praise, worship, joy, surrender
Meeting of needs, mine and others	Worship and praise	God-centred, listening	Relationship with God
Less nervous, more self-control	Manifesting fruit of the Spirit	Others seek their counsel	Controlled by Spirit, live at peace with others
Secure, optimistic	Secure, confident	Deepening peacefulness	Strong faith, optimistic, deep trust

FOR FURTHER THOUGHT

1 Joanna's faith had grown, while Rachel felt hers
   had not. Which of them do you identify with,
   and why?
2 If your faith is growing, can you do as Joanna did
   and help a friend whose spiritual journey seems
   to be in hiatus?
3 If your faith isn't growing, can you see why?
   What steps can you take to start growing in faith
   again?

Notes

1 Briscoe, Jill, *Hush! Hush! It's time to pray – but how?*
   (Glasgow: Pickering & Inglis, 1978), p. 9.
2 Some examples are the well-known Alpha Course,
   the Emmaus Course, Just Looking, or the Y Course.
3 Christian Research, *Congregational Attitudes and Beliefs
   Survey*, private research.
4 Ibid.
5 Ocho, Carol, *Women and Spirituality* (New Jersey:
   Rowman & Allanhel, 1983), p. 5.
6 Engel, James F., *Contemporary Christian Communications* (Nashville and New York: Thomas Nelson,
   1975), p. 83.
7 This version from Drane, John, *Evangelism for a New
   Age*, (London: Marshall Pickering, 1994), p. 202 and
   Brierley, Peter, *Reaching and Keeping Teenagers* (Tun-
   bridge Wells: MARC and London: Christian Research, London, 1993), p. 158.
8 Martin, Glen S. and Ginter, Dian, *Drawing Closer*
   (Nashville: Broadman & Holman, 1995), pp. 21–7.

9

Greener Grass

'I think it's about time I went back to church again,' Chris remarked one evening when she and Joanna had been praying together.

Joanna was delighted. 'What's made you come to that decision?' she enquired.

'Well, mostly us praying together. I thought I was doing OK without church. I still believe in everything I believed in when I went, but it's marvellous having the space to do what I want when I want at the weekend. Sometimes down by the river I'm overwhelmed by a sense of the presence of God.'

She paused, and Joanna waited. After a moment or two, Chris continued thoughtfully, 'Gradually I've realized that knowing God is with me by the river isn't quite the same as feeling his presence in a group of people. I miss the singing too – you know, unless you belong to a choir, there's hardly anywhere else where people sing together, except perhaps down the pub when they're drunk, or before football matches. Neither of those are really my scene!'

They laughed together.

'So, what's us praying together had to do with it?' asked Joanna.

'When we first started I wasn't sure whether I really wanted to do it, but I did want your friendship. What surprised me was that you didn't judge me at all when I told you why I'd stopped going to church, and you believed me when I said I still believed in God and everything. So I thought it wouldn't do any harm to say yes when you suggested praying together, if that's what you wanted. But then, as we prayed more regularly, I realized I was pretty dry spiritually. I suppose I haven't been feeding my spirit in any significant way. I've begun to realize that my faith is still very important to me, and if it's important I need to do something about it. I want to meet with a group of people who share my faith and who see life in a similar way. It looks as if the best way to do that is to start going to church again.'

'Would you like to come with us?' Joanna queried.

'No, I don't think so,' Chris said, hesitantly. 'It isn't that I don't want to worship with you, but I think I need to go somewhere where I can be a bit anonymous at first. I can't do that round here, because too many people know me or knew my parents. I thought I might start by going into the city and trying some churches there. The thing is that long-term, I want somewhere where I could get involved again – perhaps start using my teaching skills in some way. That means I need to go to a church which lets women use their gifts. In all your reading, Joanna, have you found out how different denominations feel about women, especially ones that want to use their gifts?'

Joanna admitted that she hadn't considered that so far. She suggested that both of them see what they could find out from books and by exploring the Internet. She was delighted that Chris wanted to come back to church but didn't want to rush her into going somewhere where she would feel uncomfortable.

*   *   *   *   *

There are significant differences between denominations on issues relating to women. These particularly apply to women as ministers, but attitudes are often reflected in the wider life of the church. Many women are unaware of these differences, and assume that other churches are like their own.

Why the difference?

It would be easy to argue that because theological discussion originates with the Bible we should be able to agree on what it teaches. Unfortunately it is not so simple – would that it were!

There are very divergent theologies about the role of women in the church which have also been applied to church life in very different ways. Take, for example, the variety of opinions among those who consider that the Bible excludes women from certain public, upfront roles in the church. That is about the only thing they agree on! Some deny women almost any role at all, expecting them to remain silent in church other than to sing the hymns. Then there are churches which allow women to take a normal part in church life, but not to take any sort

of leadership or teaching role, except perhaps in
Sunday School. Rachel's vicar was like that. In other
churches women are allowed to speak and teach,
but only under the authority of a man, so she might
be one of a team of leaders, but not number one. Yet
another view allows a woman to be in charge of a local church, as long as she is under the authority of a
male bishop. Another view, held by many of those
who see ministers as priests, is to believe that because a woman cannot represent Christ, she should
not celebrate the eucharist.[1] Alongside are those
who in theory state that a woman can take a leadership role in church, but in practice prefer to limit
them to 'traditional' women's roles of work among
women and children.

The difficulties are made worse by the biblical pas-
sages, which are quoted by various sides in the argument, being notoriously difficult to interpret and open
to a range of readings. Groups at opposite ends of the
discussion may use the same passage of Scripture to
back up their position. This book is not about biblical
interpretation, but if you are concerned about the issue
a number of writers have addressed it.[2]

Specific denominations

With the proviso that situations change, let's take a
quick canter through the main denominational positions (recognizing that there are always exceptions
to every rule) looking at the kind of issues that Chris
and Joanna might have been searching for information about.

Anglican churches

This description includes the Church of England, Church in Wales, Church of Ireland, Episcopal Church of Scotland, and other episcopal churches within the Anglican Communion around the world.

The General Synod of the Church of England voted in 1992 to allow the ordination of women as priests, and the first were ordained in 1994. They had been allowed to be deaconesses since the 1860s, but that position didn't let them preside at the eucharist (or communion). The arguments for and against ordaining women as priests raged long and hard, and a measure of the depth of feeling is reflected in the numbers of clergy and members of congregations who left the Church of England after the vote. Some became Roman Catholics and a few joined one of the branches of the Orthodox church. Others remained Anglicans, but not within the Church of England, while two groups remained within the Church of England but disagreed loudly with the decision.[3] All churches had to vote on what they wanted to do locally about women priests, and so-called 'flying bishops' were appointed to provide oversight for churches not wanting anything to do with women priests. One or two women have been 'promoted' to archdeacon or provost of a cathedral.

However, the Church of England's debate about whether to allow women to become bishops still has a long way to run, although the July 2000 General Synod voted to set up a theological commission to consider the issues raised if women were appointed bishops.

Other Anglican churches in the United Kingdom
are at different stages along a similar path, while Anglican churches elsewhere in the world are divided
on the issue. In other Western nations a number of
women bishops have been appointed,[4] while the
rapidly growing Anglican churches in Africa are
mostly outspokenly against them.

This book has not been primarily about women in
leadership roles, so why all this detail about women
priests? Someone recently said to me,

> The Church of England thinks it has solved the problem
> for women by allowing women to be ordained. While it
> may have helped those women, it has done almost
> nothing for the position of ordinary women in the pew.

However, other pressures on the church are having
the indirect effect of allowing women more freedom
to exercise their gifts. Although more men and
women are entering the ministry than in recent
years, there are not enough to replace the large numbers retiring. Parishes now have to pay pensions for
clergy, which were formerly paid by the Church
Commissioners. This, combined with the massive
number of listed buildings to be maintained,[5]
stretches church resources enormously.

A range of measures designed to make much
better use of lay people is trying to compensate for
these demands. These often allow more scope for
women. There's a large army of Readers and a
growth of Locally Ordained Ministers (people li-
censed as a minister only within their own parish).

Some dioceses train evangelists, while others have significant numbers of Non-Stipendiary Ministers (people who are ordained, but work in another paid job rather than as a parish priest). In these groups of officially recognized ministry there are many women who, for a whole range of reasons, do not wish to become full priests, but have found an outlet for using their gifts in the service of God and the church. At the lay level, there are many women churchwardens, and on average half of PCC members are women.[6]

Virtually all the major denominations have at least one women's organization as part of their church life. The Episcopal Church Women within the Episcopal Church USA (the main American Anglican church) illustrates well the aims of many of these organizations:

Vision Statement

> We are Episcopal Church Women, committed to one another and called to be witnesses for Christ.
> Our challenge is to provide a safe place where every person is free to become the person Christ created her to be.
> We are called. We are different. We are one body.
> *Purpose*
> The purpose of this organization shall be to assist the women of the Episcopal Church to carry on Christ's work of reconciliation in the world and to take their place as leaders in the life, governance and worship of the church.

Who We Are

Women of all ages, ethnic origins, socioeconomic back-
grounds in the Episcopal Church USA, who choose
to participate.[7]

The Roman Catholic Church

The Catholic Church has always simultaneously
limited the ministry of women and given them enormous opportunities. Women cannot become priests
and lead a local congregation, and in spite of various
movements around the world this is unlikely to
change in the immediate future. The issue of
whether male priests must continue to remain celibate is expected to take priority over the priesting of
women.[8]

However, the religious orders have given considerable scope to women for hundreds of years, with
women's orders of nuns exercising a very wide
range of ministry outside local church leadership.
They have provided countless thousands of women
(as well as men) with opportunities for independence from their family, and leadership in their own
sphere. They have founded hospitals, schools and
missionary orders, and despite diminishing numbers in most countries, continue to provide many
women with a fulfilling way of serving God and the
church. As we've already seen, the Reformation actually limited the ministry of protestant women by
removing from them the possibility of serving in a
religious order, although Anglicans, Lutherans and
a few other denominations have re-instated them.

The Pope surprised many observers and encouraged women by a statement in 1995 about women's role in the church. In that statement he affirmed the dignity and value of women, reminded people that Christianity has always attracted more women than men, and underlined that difference between men and women 'does not mean an inevitable and almost implacable opposition'. He went on to say that the 'renewal of the temporal order can only come about by the co-operation of men and women'.[9]

A statement by the Catholic Bishops of England and Wales in 1980 has been much quoted by Catholic women's organizations, which offer women a forum for debating the issues of women's ministry in the Catholic church. It read:

> We believe the time is overdue for more positive attitudes about your participation in the life of the Church and we recognize with regret that you have often been permitted to play mainly a limited, and often inferior, part in the Church.' They went on to say, 'We assure you of our collaboration and support as you achieve your genuine role in the Church and society at large.[10]

Orthodox Churches

There are many strands of the Orthodox Church, with major groupings such as Russian, Greek, Coptic and Syrian Orthodox. Their numbers in the UK are small, although they were one of the few denominations which grew in the 1990s, doubling their numbers from 12,300 to 25,200.[11] Their theologies vary slightly, but on the role of women they hold a very similar position to the Roman Catholic church.

Methodists

From their earliest days the Methodists have allowed women to take leadership positions. John Wesley, the founder of Methodism, taught widely the 'priesthood of all believers', which operated as a great leveller of people, regardless of class, education or gender. He established a system of 'classes' to teach new converts, which suitably gifted women were allowed to lead from the earliest days. He also encouraged women who could preach to do so. One of these was Mary Bosanquet, to whom Wesley wrote: 'I think the case rests here, in your having an extraordinary call. So, I am persuaded, has every one of our lay preachers; otherwise I could not countenance his preaching at all.'[12]

Methodists organize groups of local churches into administrative units called 'circuits'. These have ministers attached, though there are not necessarily enough ministers for each church to have its own. This system deliberately means that local churches are dependent upon the involvement of local lay people as upon ordained ministers. Working hand-in-hand with the ministers – including women since 1973 – are lay preachers. Women are given complete freedom within this lay preacher system, and ministers have to be a local preacher before they can be accepted for training. It is fairly common for women who feel they have a gift of preaching but cannot exercise it in their own denomination to choose to join a Methodist church.

I deliberately chose a Methodist for one of the in-depth interviews in this research. When I asked her what other denominations can learn from Methodists, she replied:

'Equality of everyone is not something to be frightened of, the women won't suddenly take over everything. Women are given more responsibility than in most other denominations, and it works! Women with deep faith, visionary leadership skills, team players, and good speakers are given opportunities. Our dependency on the laity because of the circuit system is not just made up, we really need it'.

The Salvation Army

The Salvation Army was founded in 1865 by William *and* Catherine Booth, and right from its beginning was egalitarian. Indeed, Catherine Booth wrote a pamphlet in 1859 entitled *Female Ministry, or Women's Right to Preach the Gospel*.[13] Her argument for a woman's right to be involved fully in preaching and teaching was carefully argued both from a biblical and a natural perspective. In language that seems quaint today but which clearly made her point, she wrote:

Why should woman be confined exclusively to the kitchen and the distaff, any more than man to the field and workshop? Did not God, and has not nature, assigned to man *his* sphere of labour, 'to till the ground and to dress it?' And, if exemption is claimed from this kind of toil for a portion of the male sex, on the ground of their possessing ability for intellectual and moral pursuits, we must be allowed to claim the same privilege for women; nor can we see the exception more *unnatural* in the one case than in the other, or why God in this solitary instance has endowed a being with powers which He never intended her to employ.[14]

Throughout its history the Salvation Army has given women equal responsibility alongside its men, in leading local corps, getting involved in their social programmes, and rising through the ranks to senior leadership. Their General in the early 1990s was an Australian woman, Eva Burrows, and they now have more female officers in the UK than male!

Baptists

Baptist churches tend to be more independent than most of the other major denominations. So it was possible for Baptists in England and Wales to allow a women to be given pastoral charge of a church in 1918 and for the Bristol Baptist College to agree in 1919 to accept women for training, although none did so until 1927. However, Baptists in Scotland permitted churches to appoint a woman minister only in 1999. Local churches decide for themselves whether to allow women to be deacons, or elders if they have them. On the other hand, it was a Baptist who wrote the book *Leadership is Male*![15]

Church of Scotland

The first women were ordained ministers in the Church of Scotland in 1969 with very little fuss or difficulty. They seem to have been accepted as a normal part of church life, with women ministers not facing particular problems that are different from men's.

House or New Churches

There are many varieties of house churches, which these days are more often termed New Churches. Their position on women varies enormously. Some of the so-called 'streams' (they don't like to be called a denomination) allow considerable freedom for women. An example of this is Ichthus Christian Fellowship, which is led equally by Roger and Faith Forster. Faith is a frequent speaker, nationwide, on issues of women and leadership. Women in Ichthus are treated equally on the basis of their ability and gifting, with some of their congregations being led by women.[16]

Another of the in-depth interviewees was a house church leader. She takes a more conservative position than Ichthus, although still open, and told me:

'In house churches men have greater opportunities to use their gifts without restrictions. This is part of British culture, and part of church culture too. There are major opportunities for women, but there are still restrictions, so someone may ask, 'Do you think as a woman you should be doing this?' Men's instinct is to ask this, especially when facing a very difficult situation; it's part of their protective instinct. It's seen as more 'normal' for a man to lead, but this shouldn't exclude women who have a gifting for it'.

At the other end of the scale, some house church streams still do not have women leaders, and restrict women's teaching mainly to other women or children.

Christian Brethren

The Brethren traditionally have not appointed ministers, their services being led by locally appointed elders. These were always men, and women were not allowed to speak in their unstructured services. The Exclusive Brethren continue this position, but many of the other Assemblies, as their churches are known, now style themselves as Independent Evangelical Churches. Some have appointed ministers, or at least full-time elders, and many have relaxed their rules about women's public involvement in services.[17]

Pentecostal churches, especially Assemblies of God

The Pentecostal religious movement began in the early twentieth century during a spiritual revival when gifts of the Holy Spirit were manifested by men and women, particularly through speaking in tongues. Therefore right from the movement's inception the giftings of the Holy Spirit were seen, at least in theory, as being open to be exercised by both men and women. This was officially agreed at a major convention in Sunderland in 1914. The Assemblies of God movement was founded in 1924 and from the beginning several women were accepted onto the ministerial list. However, the practice hasn't always quite matched the theory.

In 1995, 105 out of the 635 full-time pastors within the Assemblies of God in Britain responded to a survey about the role of women in the church.[18] 12 of them disagreed with the statement that 'women should have exactly the same opportunities for ministry as men', and 18 agreed that 'women should *not* be in charge of congregations'. (Italics mine.)

The survey also asked about the greatest contribution made by women to the life of the local church. Prayer came out by far the strongest with 60% of votes, while practical areas were second with 29%. Evangelistic and pastoral work by women was rated much less important. However, other aspects of the survey showed that pastors put a strong emphasis on a woman taking a traditional role in the home, and specifically that she should 'obey her husband' (92% of pastors agreed with this). Perhaps family and children thus take priority to the exclusion of time or energy for evangelistic and pastoral work.

United Reformed Church

This denomination was formed in 1972 by the union of the Congregational Church in England and Wales with the Presbyterian Church in England. It is a very democratic and egalitarian denomination, and women have played as full a part in the life and ministry of the church as they wish to, right from its inception.

* * * * *

Joanna and Chris met again a couple of weeks later to share what they had found out. They were surprised how much information they'd been able to unearth. They read it through together and ruled out one or two denominations for Chris. She wanted somewhere where she could feel free to use her gifts in teaching, if the opportunity arose sometime in the future. They pored over the telephone directory and a map of the city, trying to work out which denominations had churches which were easily accessible by car, and that ruled out a few more.

In the end, Chris looked at Joanna and said, 'This isn't going to decide it for me. It helps, but I need to find a place where I'm made welcome and believe I can feel at home. This information isn't going to tell me that! These addresses are more useful. I think on Saturday I'll drive in and have a look at some of them, and make up my mind then which to try on Sunday – I guess that will depend on whether they've got a notice board that gives the times of the services!'

FOR FURTHER THOUGHT

1 How much does the attitude towards women in your church reflect the denomination to which the church belongs? How much is it affected by individuals in your church?

2 If the position of women in your local church is a real problem for you, would you consider changing denomination, like Chris is doing?

Notes

1 Men and women in the church', *Themelios*, 4/87, p. 87.
2 See, for example, the following books, many of which have a bibliography listing other books on the subject:
Evans, Mary, *Woman in the Bible* (Carlisle: Paternoster, 1983).
Hurley, James, *Man and Woman in Biblical Perspective* (Nottingham: IVP, 1981).
Langley, Myrtle S., *Equal Women: A Christian Feminist Perspective* (London: Marshalls, 1983).
Lees, Shirley (ed.), *The Role of Women* (Nottingham: IVP, 1984).
Lutz, Lorry, *Women as Risk-Takers for God* (Carlisle: WEF in association with Paternoster, 1997).
Martin, Joan (ed.), *The Ladies Aren't For Silence* (Milton Keynes: Word, 1991).
Noble, Christine, *What in the World is God Saying About Women?* (Eastbourne: Kingsway, 1990).
Storkey, Elaine, *Created or Constructed: The Great Gender Debate* (Carlisle: Paternoster, 2000).
Storkey, Elaine, *What's Right with Feminism?* (London: SPCK, 1985).
3 Gould, Peter, 'Alternative Anglicanism', *Religious Trends 1998/1999* (London: Christian Research and Carlisle: Paternoster, 1997), pp. 2, 18.
4 The first English woman to be appointed bishop was Penny Jamieson, who is Bishop of Dunedin on New Zealand's South Island.

5   Brierley, Peter, *The Tide is Running Out* (London: Christian Research, 2000), p. 205.

6   Christian Research, *Women in the Christian Community*, survey of Christian Research Association members, 1996.

7   Leaflet produced by Episcopal Church Women, Episcopal Church USA, 1995.

8   e.g. The Rt Revd Guazzelli, retired bishop in East London, writing in *Catholic Herald*, 23 June 2000.

9   Reported in Kenny, Mary, 'Why the Pope said he was sorry', *Daily Telegraph*, July 12 1995 and *Agenda for the Third Millennium*, Alan Neame (trans.) (London: Fount, 1996), pp. 48-52.

10 Quoted widely, e.g. in Cosstick, Vicky, 'The role of women in the Church', and Pratt, Oliver and Ianthe, 'Women in the Church', *The Sower*, Winter 1987/9, Vol. 11, No. 2.

11 Brierley, *The Tide is Running Out*, p. 34.

12 Langley, Myrtle S., 'Attitudes to Women in the British Churches' in Paul Badham (ed.), *Religion, State and Society in Modern Britain* (Lampeter: The Edwin Mellen Press, 1989), p. 298.

13 Booth, Catherine, *Female Ministry, or Women's Right to Preach the Gospel* (London: Chase and Morgan, 1859, reprinted by the Salvation Army Supplies Printing and Publishing Department, New York, 1975).

14 Ibid. p. 5.

15 Pawson, David, *Leadership is Male* (Guildford: Highland Books, 1994).

16 e.g. Fran Beckett, who is Chief Executive of the Shaftesbury Society, is also joint leader of an Ichthus congregation in South London.

17 See Rogers, Olive, 'Role and Contribution of Women in the Church' in Rowden, Harold H. (ed.), *Strengthening Local Churches* (Carlisle: Partnership with Paternoster, 1993), p. 73.

18 Kay, William K. and Robbins, Mandy, *A Woman's Place is on her knees – the pastor's view of the role of women in the Assemblies of God*, undated paper, Centre for Theology and Education, Trinity College, Carmarthen.

10

Go For It!

The aim of this research was summed up as *wanting to encourage women to play as active a part as possible in the life of their local church.* How can this happen? The research showed that change is needed in three areas: national church institutions, local churches and their leaders, and within women themselves.

National church institutions

Structures

This research project shows that most ordinary churchgoing women, who are rarely very vocal on the subject, nevertheless feel fairly strongly that the use of women's gifts in the church should not be limited by their gender but only by their ability. They may not wish to be ordained themselves, but find it difficult to accept that in some Christian churches a suitably gifted woman cannot be ordained.

One of the roots of this feeling is a general sense of dissatisfaction that church institutions remain very masculine, not only in their hierarchical structures, but also in attitudes towards women working within those structures. Perhaps a good example is seen in this description of the appointment of Angela Sarkis to lead one of the Church of England's national organizations:

> Her appointment as Chief Executive of the Church Urban Fund worried some, shocked a few and filled the visionary with a sense of excitement. She was, after all, a rank outsider in every sense of the word: a woman in secular employment, a Pentecostal and black. The Church Urban Fund, like almost all of the Church of England, had always been managed by white, middle- or vaguely upper-class males.[1]

Perhaps all denominations could do with a few more like Angela Sarkis – women who will rattle the cages of the masculine structures and help open them up to the feminine perspective. After all, more than half of church attenders are women – what commercial organization could afford to downplay half their customers?

The Lausanne Committee for World Evangelization have a Senior Associate for Women who works internationally. The appointment came about as a result of the women's track at Lausanne II in Manila in 1989. During the discussions, which involved over 1,000 men and women from around the world, they considered the key issues for women in ministry and mission:

We concluded our track with a recognition of the need
to train today's women for tomorrow's task and realized that this will involve churches providing theological and practical training for women, as well as
encouraging them in the ministries they already
shared.[2]

There are many more such opportunities for women
in Britain than in some other parts of the world, but
more could be done, especially at Diocesan and re-
gional level, to encourage and make it easier for
women to take advantage of the openings that already exist.

Attitudes

Many denominational attitudes filter down from the
top. Denominations can easily become so caught up
with the issues surrounding women in ministry –
can they be ordained, should they lead a local congregation alone, will they be allowed to take more senior roles, etc. – that they overlook or lay aside the
concerns of the majority of women. Most women
churchgoers don't want to be ordained. They may
not even want an upfront leadership role in their
own congregation. They would simply like to be recognized for and encouraged in what they do. This
could, and perhaps should, begin by a change of attitude at a national level. Stuart Briscoe, pastor and
speaker, commented:

Unfortunately, the church has not always recognized
the spiritual giftedness of women . . . This is not only an

insult to the Spirit but is also a great hindrance to the work of the church as many vital members of the body are not functioning optimally. I believe that an effort must be made on the part of the leadership of all churches to come to some agreement as to the optimum way in which women's ministry is acceptable and should be encouraged. Even if, for theological or other reasons, it is felt that limits should be put on what women are allowed to do, this should not mean that there should not be careful thought and encouragement given to women to do all that they possibly can do.[3]

Wider opportunities

Women are looking for a wider range of opportunities in which to serve their local church, and through which to serve God. Some enjoy arranging flowers or making tea, and would like to be recognized for doing it well. Others may have significant responsibility at work and find it hard to understand why the church does not seem to want to benefit from their gifts and experience.

Gerard Kelly points out that this is particularly true of the young people who are still within the church:

Whatever your take on gender and leadership, there can be no doubt that many of the attributes of controlling leadership have been, over the centuries, predominantly male characteristics, and that the 'resourceful friends' model has a more feminine ethos. If the twenty-first century is to have the leaders it is crying out for, then it is clear that more of them must be women, and that those that are not must adopt a more gender-balanced approach. This is an insight recognised, and welcomed, by many in the rising generations, with a growing commitment to see a more balanced view of leadership, both in terms of the skills employed and of the gender of those employing them.[4]

These wider opportunities will partly come about naturally if attitudes change. Gifted women in our churches only need the door to be opened a crack, and they will do the rest of the work.

Today bright women in our churches pour their lives into trivia, partly because they are uneasy about getting involved in significant big issues, lest they usurp the prerogative of men.[5]

Local churches and their leaders

Women would like to be able to use their gifts in the local church. However, very often the predominant culture in the congregation militates against it. They may be willing, for example, to stand for election to the PCC or diaconate, but find that no woman ever gets elected. Lorry Lutz, who has worked with local evangelical churches around the world, writes about her observations which would seem from this research to be true in other (UK and non-evangelical) churches also:

1.   An increasing number of Christian leaders want to help women develop and use their gifts in ministry. However, the tension between those who believe women should use their gifts in decision- and policy-making, and those who do not, remains high.

2.   The theological position on the biblical role of women will continue to be the major determinant as to what roles women are allowed to play in the church. Hopefully there will be more open discussion and willingness to consider new paradigms by Christian leaders.

3.   Changes in the role of women in the church are irreversible. No matter what theological position a church takes, it must cater in some way to the educated, qualified, gifted and experienced 21st century woman who has gained so much in the marketplace.[6]

She goes on to say,

Critical mass regarding women's ability freely to use their gifts in the church has not yet been reached. But, as we've seen, more and more men of God are recognizing the importance of women's gifts, and are promoting their use.[7]

This is a worldwide perspective. In Britain we do seem to have reached a point where 'critical mass' is either here, or will be very soon. Were women to withdraw their labour in protest against their working conditions, churches would actually grind to a halt very quickly. However, a church is a community of people, not a workplace, and women are committed to that community.

While men organize society, women build community, and however well the organizing is done, if there is no community the whole thing falls apart. Local churches need their women, or they will die.

What women want from a local church will vary:

> Older people are more loyal to their church, and also tend to be more set in their ways. They may not want to take on new roles themselves, but nevertheless they may be delighted to see their daughters and grand-daughters given the opportunities they never had.
>
> Women in their middle years are often juggling a wide range of responsibilities with family and work. However, many of them would like to be respected and valued for who they are. They may be able to take on a specific role in the church, particularly if its demands can be tailored to meet their limitations e.g. meeting a little later in the evening so there is time to cook and eat between getting in from work and going out again.
>
> Younger women are likely to only be part of the church, let alone involved in it more deeply, as the result of conscious choice. They are more likely to want to give the limited time they have available to activities which 'make a difference', and when the need is met or their interests change, they will move on to something or somewhere else. Churches need to be flexible enough to use the gifts of these younger women – if we don't keep them in the church now, we won't have any older women left to lead in a few years' time![8]

But use of gifts is far from being the only issue for women. Their role in holding the church together is a vital one. The relationships which women build and nurture is what keeps many people in the church. The sense of community and belonging which is so vital to women already in the church is often what attracts others to join. A woman's perspective on faith is different in some respects from a man's, and enriches the spiritual life of the church.

The plea of women in this research project is that these major contributions to church life are recognized and affirmed. They'd like to be valued for who they are, and acknowledged – even thanked occasionally! – for what they do. Indeed, part of the role of Robyn Claydon, the Senior Associate for Women appointed following Lausanne II in Manila, is to 'Endeavour by a variety of means to encourage all women in the work they are doing for the Lord.'[9]

Women themselves

We women can be our own worst enemies! Sometimes, the opportunities are there, but we won't take them. A survey on behalf of Ecumenical Women in Scotland found that:

> Several respondents reported that in their own Churches there was equality between genders. This was expressed as equality of opportunity. Opportunity where offered, however, is not always taken up . . . It was taken as understood by some participants that for the traditional structure of authority to change, it must be women themselves who decide to take an active part in changing it. This was seen as a question of realising their own potential and taking an active role, rather than passively waiting for permission to be given.[10]

Even some of the women who offer for ordination
may be doing so to create opportunities for their own
ministry which they might have been able to exercise
in other ways had they had the courage to do so.
Penny Jamieson, in her book *Living at the Edge*, comments:

> There is clear evidence from my own experience, both
> of myself and of other women, that there does tend to be
> a diffidence and even anxiety within many women
> about assuming authority . . . It is clear to me that one of
> the reasons why more women are seeking ordination is
> that they feel the need for authorization, the 'received'
> authority that the institution can bestow, in order to
> function effectively. It is frequently hard for women to
> move from their gratitude at being granted authority
> by the institution to a clearer sense of who they are, and
> to the authority that comes from being who they are . . . I
> would like to see more lay women claiming that author-
> ity without benefit of ordination.[11]

Women and authority is a very sensitive issue. Without it, it is hard for women to take any initiative. If they
do, they are accused of being power hungry. But without some sort of public recognition or affirmation,
they are hamstrung. One woman interviewed in the
research had been appointed diocesan training officer
and commented how wonderful it was to walk into a
church with an official position and to be welcomed
and recognized as such. It gave her confidence. However, someone else who was an official church visitor
and counsellor didn't know whether she was over-
stepping her position if she was in the foyer saying

goodbye to people as they left. It helped her to contact people, but she felt that some people thought she was trespassing on the minister's patch. Deep down, she felt uncertain and did not want to be misunderstood. It seems that somehow women are always looking over their shoulder trying to avoid giving offence.

A recent secular book, *The New Feminism* by Natasha Walters, points out that while most women eschew the word 'feminist', they have, in fact, taken on board much of today's feminist agenda in terms of justice, equal pay, no discrimination etc. As more and more Christian women work outside the home, this will probably be increasingly true. Before some women can take the opportunities for which they are gifted and which may be open to them, they may need to confront deeper issues concerning their own personality or experience. This can be painful, but for many people it is a necessary part of maturing in the Christian life.

Relationships are the glue

Women may not either want nor be able to take an obvious leadership role in their local church, but nurturing, caring for and supporting others is vital to the life of the congregation.

For many women their Christian life revolves around relationships:

- They often come to church to worship *with* people.

- If they are tempted not to go on a particular day they nevertheless turn up because of the people they will let down by not being there.
- Should they leave it is likely to be because a relationship has broken down, either within the church, perhaps with the minister or a colleague with whom they have been working, or within their family, so making it difficult for them to face people.
- Many older people (not only women) come to church because it is where they have found a sense of belonging and identity after the death of a spouse.
- Often, women are brought to church as newcomers through the encouragement of a friend.
- One of the reasons their faith grows is seeing God at work in others – their family or friends.
- Their faith as a relationship with God has priority over their knowledge about him.

One of the key questions which many people ask – theologians, denominational and local church leaders, and thinking Christians who are concerned about the future of the church in the UK – is, 'What is church?' Part of the emerging answer is that, when many other community-based structures and institutions are falling apart, it is more important than ever that the church should demonstrate the reality of a loving and caring community. In the years ahead, the communal aspect of the life of a local church is likely to be one of its key functions. If this is even partly true, women will have a significant part to play in helping to build communities in local churches.[12]

Let's go for it and be the glue that helps to hold the church community together!

Notes

1   Guinness, Michele, *Is God Good For Women?* (London: Hodder & Stoughton, 1997), p. 231.

2   Douglas, J.D. (ed.), *Proclaim Christ Until He Comes* (Minneapolis: World Wide Publications, 1989), p. 396.

3   Stuart Briscoe, quoted in Lutz, Lorry, *Women as Risk-Takers for God* (Carlisle: WEF in association with Paternoster, 1997), p. 253.

4   Kelly, Gerard, *Get a Grip on the Future Without Losing Your Hold on the Past* (London: Monarch, 2000), p. 250.

5   Adeney, Miriam, quoted in Nixson, Rosie, *Liberating Women for the Gospel* (London: Hodder & Stoughton, 1997), p. 28.

6   Lutz, *Women as Risk-Takers for God*, p. 255.

7   Ibid. p. 260.

8   Church of Scotland Woman's Guild Research and Development Project, *20/20 Vision* (Edinburgh: St Andrew Press), p. 53.

9   Douglas, *Proclaim Christ Until He Comes*, p. 397.

10   Hart, Margaret, *To Have a Voice* (Edinburgh: Saint Andrew Press, 1995), pp. 26–7, on behalf of Network of Ecumenical Women in Scotland.

11   Jamieson, Penny, *Living at the Edge*, (London: Mowbray, 1997), p. 138.

12   Drane, John, *The McDonaldization of the Church* (London: Darton, Longman & Todd, 2000), p.161

Postscript

Having reached the end of this book you may be wondering what happened to Joanna, Rachel and Chris. They are fictional characters I created to illustrate the findings of the research. So how about *you* deciding what happened to them? None of them will reflect your situation exactly, but the process of thinking through how their story could develop might help you to think about how your own spiritual journey could move on. Here are a few ideas to get you started.

→ Joanna is now on the PCC as well as sometimes leading Bible study in her home group. How will these activities help her faith to grow? What might she move on to next?

→ As Stephen gets more involved with youth work, what pressures and opportunities might that create for other members of the family?

→ How can Stephen and Joanna encourage their children's faith to grow in the years ahead?

→ How might Chris and Joanna's friendship develop?

→ What sort of church do you think Chris will settle in and why? How might her faith grow as part of that church?

→ What should Rachel say to Mike when she gets home from the weekend away? What action might they take about their church situation?

→ In five years' time why might the vicar be glad that Joanna and Stephen chose his church?

→ Daydream a bit . . . what might be happening to these characters in ten years' time?

→ And for yourself . . . in what areas would you like your faith to grow? Would you like to use your gifts in new ways – if so, how? Where do you hope your spiritual journey will take you in the next ten years?

You could answer these questions on your own, with a group of friends or women in your church, or in a home group. If you would be interested in attending a study day based on the findings of this research, contact Heather Wraight at:

Christian Research
Vision Building
4 Footscray Road
Eltham
London
SE9 2TZ

E-mail: admin@christian-research.org.uk

Methodology

Organisation

The research was planned by a steering committee of women who represented a wide range of denominational and church organizations.

Members of the Steering Committee

Mrs Sarah Finch	Chair, board member of the Bible Society
Renira Branscombe	Mothers' Union
Captain Wendy Caffull	The Salvation Army
Jill Garrett	Gallup
Valerie Griffiths	Women Reaching Women
Margaret Killingray	London Institute for Contemporary Christianity
Sister Stella Noons	Church Army (replaced by Catherine Wellingbrook)
Sue Plater	Christian Aid
Liz Trundle	Woman Alive
Revd Anne Wright	Church Pastoral Aid Society

In addition there was a wider group of some forty women who acted as an advisory board. They were invited to planning meetings at key points during the project, and kept informed of developments throughout.

Scale of the project

The original aim was a large-scale survey exploring the differences between men and women in their attitudes, needs and expectations in relation to the church. Unfortunately, despite considerable effort, it proved impossible to raise sufficient funds.

The committee decided to go ahead with as much as the available funding would allow. This proved to be three focus groups, in-depth interviews with six women from different areas of Christian experience but each with a nationwide perspective, and a review of the literature already existing on the subject. It was always intended that the results would be produced in book form, as well as examined through seminars or study days.

Issues for research

The aim of the research was to consider the ordinary woman in the pew, rather than women in positions of local church leadership (ministers, pastors, vicars etc.). At the time the research was being initiated, Christian Research was piloting a survey called the Congregational Attitudes and Beliefs Survey

(CABS). This survey was designed to be completed by all members of a local congregation, and has since been repeated on a wider scale. The pilots were run in churches of five denominations. For the purpose of the women's research, the responses to these pilots were analysed by gender and note taken of matters where in at least three of the churches the replies of men and women were statistically significantly different. These issues then formed the basis of the discussions in the focus groups and in-depth interviews.

In-depth interviews

Six women were chosen, each with some kind of national role, though not in local church leadership. Each was interviewed for one and a half hours, discussing the same issues as the focus groups. The steering committee is most grateful to these women for taking part:

> Canon Dr Christina Baxter, Principal, St John's College, Nottingham. Also chaired the Ecumenical Debate of Solidarity with Women.

> Jane Collins, co-publisher of Monarch Publications and editor of *Wholeness* magazine.

> Pat Cook, international missions co-ordinator for Pioneer churches, and regular speaker at events and conferences for women.

> Jacqui Frost, Director of Lantern Arts Centre, who works extensively with her husband Rob in leading events such as Easter People.

Michele Guinness, author of *Is God Good for Women?* plus other works, and wife of an Anglican vicar.

Jenny Joice, former director of The Cog Wheel Trust, an organization providing counselling and therapy for individuals, families and couples, and offering marriage preparation. Also a member of Singularly Significant, a former Evangelical Alliance coalition.

Two of the women who attended a focus group and who represented the general experience of women in those groups were also interviewed in depth. The members of the steering committee each gave their personal response to the questions posed in the focus groups. In addition, during the period of this research, I have personally explored the issues covered by it in numerous private conversations with friends and other contacts.

Focus groups

Three were held, one in a suburban area of London, one in a rural area of Kent and one in the town of Worthing. These locations were chosen for their different social environments, and the availability of women from a range of denominations. The small number of focus groups showed remarkable similarities in their findings, which suggests that further groups would probably not have provided any substantially different results.

Literature

The Christian Research library contains many research projects on a wide range of subjects. It is widely seen as a resource by the media and researchers. Most of the books and research papers quoted in this book were found in the library.

Bibliography

Bede, *Ecclesiastical History of the English People*, Farmer, D.H. (ed.), Sherley-Price, Leo (trans.) (London: Penguin, 1990 revised ed.).

Booth, Catherine, *Female Ministry, or Women's Right to Preach the Gospel* (London: Chase and Morgan, 1859, reprinted by The Salvation Army Supplies Printing and Publishing Department, New York, 1975).

Brierley, Peter, *Finding Faith in 1994* (London: Christian Research, 1994).

—, *Future Church* (London: Christian Research, 2000).

—, *Reaching and Keeping Teenagers* (London: MARC Europe, 1992).

—, *Religious Trends 1998/1999* (London: Christian Research and Carlisle: Paternoster, 1997).

—, *Religious Trends 2000/2001* (London: Christian Research and HarperCollins*Religious*, 1999).

—, *Religious Trends 2002/2003* (London: Christian Research 2001).

—, *The Tide is Running Out* (London: Christian Research, 2000).

—, *Vision Building* (London: Christian Research, 1994 reprint).

—, and Wraight, Heather, (eds.), *UK Christian Handbook 1996/1997* (London: Christian Research, 1995).

—, *UK Christian Handbook 2000/2001* (London: Christian Research and HarperCollins*Religious*, 1999).

Briscoe, Jill, *Hush! Hush! It's time to pray – but how?* (Glasgow: Pickering & Inglis, 1978).

Byrne, Eileen, 'Women's Creative Role in the Church', *Zadok Paper*, Series 1, Paper S57 (Australia: Zadok Institute, 1992).

Christian Research, *Congregational Attitudes and Beliefs Survey* (pilot study 1998, and subsequent surveys).

—, *Older People and the Church* (London: Christian Research, 1999 for the Sir Halley Stewart Age Awareness Project. Now published as *Older People and the Church*, (Peterborough, Methodist Publishing House, 2001).

—, *They Call Themselves Christian* (London: Christian Research, 1999).

—, *Women in the Christian Community* (survey of Christian Research Association members, 1996).

Cosstick, Vicky, 'The role of women in the Church', *The Sower*, Winter 1987/9, Vol. 11, No. 2.

Dalton, Dorothy, *Gender and Chief Executives in the Voluntary Sector* (London: ACENVO, 1997).

Diesdendorf, Eileen, 'Why Some Bright Women Quit the Church', *Zadok Perspectives* No. 21, 3/88 (Australia: Zadok Institute, 1988).

Douglas, J. D. (ed.), *Proclaim Christ Until He Comes* (Minneapolis: World Wide Publications, 1989).

Drane, John, *Evangelism for a New Age* (London: Marshall Pickering, 1994).

—, *The McDonalidization of the Church* (London: Darton, Longman & Todd, 2000).

Engel, James F., *Contemporary Christian Communications* (Nashville and New York: Thomas Nelson, 1975).

Eurostat, *Women in the European Community* (Brussels: Eurostat, 1992).

Evans, Mary, *Women in the Bible* (Carlisle: Paternoster, 1983).

Fanstone, Michael, *The Sheep that Got Away* (Eastbourne: Monarch Publications, 1993).

Farmer, D. H. (ed.), *The Age of Bede*, Webb, J. F. (trans.) (London: Penguin, 1988 revised ed.).

Gill, Sean, *Women and the Church of England* (London: SPCK, 1994).

Gilligan, Carol, *In a Different Voice* (Cambridge, Massachusetts: Harvard University Press, 1982).

Gray, John, *Men are from Mars, Women are from Venus* (London and New York: HarperCollins, 1993).

Guiness, Michele, *Is God Good for Women?* (London: Hodder & Stoughton, 1997).

Harrison, Jan, *Attitudes to Bible, God and Church* (Swindon: Bible Society, 1983).

Hart, Margaret, *To Have a Voice* (Edinburgh: Saint Andrew Press, 1995).

Hill, Elizabeth, *Gender Inequality* (Australia: Zadok Institute, Zadok/TEAR occasional publication, undated).

Hughes, Philip, 'Nominalism in Australia' in *They Call Themselves Christian* (London: Christian Research and Lausanne Committee for World Evangelization, 1999).

Hurley, James, *Man and Woman in Biblical Perspective* (Nottingham: IVP, 1981).

Hutchinson, Mark and Campion, Edmund (eds.), *Long Patient Struggle: Studies in Australian Christianity*, Vol. 2 (Australia: The Centre for the Study of Australian Christianity, Macquarie Centre, 1994).

Jamieson, Penny, *Living at the Edge* (London: Mowbray, 1997).

Jewell, Albert (ed.), *Older People and the Church* (Peterborough: Methodist Publishing House, 2001).

Kay, William K. and Francis, Leslie J., *Drift from the Churches* (Cardiff: University of Wales Press, 1996).

Kay, William K. and Robbins, Mandy, *A woman's place is on her knees – the pastor's view of the role of women in the Assemblies of God*, undated paper by Centre for Theology and Education, Trinity College, Carmarthen.

Keay, Kathy (ed.), *Women to Women* (London: MARC and Evangelical Alliance, 1988).

Kelly, Gerard, *Get a Grip on the Future Without Losing Your Hold on the Past* (London: Monarch, 2000).

Lees, Shirley (ed.), *The Role of Women* (Nottingham: IVP, 1984).

Langley, Myrtle S., 'Attitudes to Women in the British Churches' in Badham, Paul (ed.), *Religion, State, and Society in Modern Britain* (Lampeter: The Edwin Mellen Press, 1989).

—, *Equal Women: A Christian Feminist Perspective* (London: Marshalls, 1983).

Leeuwen, Mary Stewart van, *Gender and Grace* (Nottingham: IVP, 1990).

Lutz, Lorry, *Women as Risk-Takers for God* (Carlisle: WEF in association with Paternoster, 1997).

McCloughry, Roy, 'Are Men as Religious as Women?', *Christianity*, Oct. 1999.

MARC Canada, 'Feminism and the Church', *Context*, Vol. 5, Issue 2, Oct. 1995.

Martin, David, *Tongues of Fire: The Explosion of Protestantism in Latin America* (Oxford: Basil Blackwell, 1990).

Martin, Glen S. and Ginter, Dian, *Drawing Closer* (Nashville: Broadman & Holman, 1995).

Martin, Joan (ed.), *The Ladies Aren't For Silence* (Milton Keynes: Word, 1991).

Martin Soskice, Janet, 'The Silence of the Ma'ams', *Leading Light*, Vol. 1, 1993.

Miles, Rosie, *Not in Our Name: Voices of Women who have left the Church* (Nottingham: Southwell Diocesan Social Responsibility Group, 1994).

Molitor, Brian, 'Women are here to stay', *Ethos*, Dec. 1999/Jan. 2000.

Myers, Bryant, 'Women and mission', *MARC Newsletter*, Number 93–3, Sept. 1993.

Neame, Alan (trans.), *Agenda for the Third Millennium* (London: Fount, 1996).

Neil, Stephen, *The Pelican History of the Church: A History of Christian Missions* (London: Penguin, 1986 ed.).

Nixson, Rosie, *Liberating Women for the Gospel* (London: Hodder & Stoughton, 1997).

Noble, Christine, *What in the World is God Saying About Women?* (Eastbourne: Kingsway, 1990).

Ocho, Carol, *Women and Spirituality* (New Jersey: Rowman & Allanheld, 1983).

Pawson, David, *Leadership is Male* (Guildford: Highland Books, 1994).

Petroff, Elizabeth Alvilda, 'The Mystics', *Christian History*, No. 2, 1991.

Pratt, Oliver and Ianthe, 'Women in the Church', *The Sower*, Winter 1987/9, Vol. 11, No. 2.

Puttrick, Elizabeth and Clark, Peter B. (eds.), 'Women as Teachers and Disciples in Tradition and New Religions' *Studies in Women and Religion*, Vol. 32, (New York and Lampeter: The Edwin Mellen Press, 1993).

Richter, Philip and Francis, Leslie J., *Gone but not Forgotten* (London: Darton, Longman & Todd, 1998.

Robbins, Mandy, 'A Different Voice, A Different View', *Review of Religious Research*, Vol. 40, No. 1, Sept. 1998.

Rogers, Olive, 'Role and Contribution of Women in the Church', in Rowden, Harold H. (ed.), *Strengthening Local Churches* (Carlisle: Partnership with Paternoster Press, 1993).

Schmool, Marlena and Miller, Stephen, *Women in the Jewish Community* (London: Women in the Community, 1994).

Shiels, W. J. and Wood, Diana (eds)., *Studies in Church History*, Vol. 27 (Oxford: Basil Blackwell, 1990).

Simson, Wolfgang, *Houses that Change the World: The Return of the House Churches* (Carlisle: Paternoster, 2001).

Storkey, Elaine, *Created or Constructed: The Great Gender Debate* (Carlisle: Paternoster, 2000).

—, *Henry Martyn Lecture 1994* (London: Evangelical Missionary Alliance, 1994).

—, *What's Right with Feminism?* (London: SPCK, 1985).

Tannen, Deborah, *You Just Don't Understand: Women and Men in Conversation* (London: Virago, 1992).

Themelios, 'Men and women in the church', 4/87.

Timms, Noel, *Family and Citizenship: Values in Contemporary Britain* (Aldershot: Dartmouth, 2000).

Valdez, Edna and Wright, Kim, 'What Men can Learn from Women (and Jesus) about Leadership, *Together*, Oct.-Dec. 1992.

Warner, Rob, 'Create a Church From Scratch', *Renewal*, March 1999.

Whitmarsh, Alyson, *Social Focus on Women* (London: HMSO Central Statistical Office, 1995).

Witherspoon, Sharon, 'Sex and Gender Issues', *British Social Attitudes*, report by Social and Community Planning Research (Aldershot: Gower Publishing Company Ltd., Aldershot, 1985).

Wraight, Heather, *Single, the Jesus Model* (Nottingham: Crossway, 1995).

Index